"Dr. Teasdale has written an immensely insightful book helping individuals and local churches rethink and reframe conversations around evangelism. This book provides a set of best practices as a starting point for authentic evangelism that invites people into the good news of who God is and how he is at work in the world. While written from a thoughtful theological and academic perspective, Dr. Teasdale's own personal experiences and obvious passion for evangelism make the book powerful and practical for every reader, from pastors to seminarians, church leaders and lay people."

Debi Nixon, managing executive director, The United Methodist Church of the Resurrection, Leawood, Kansas

"As one who strives to teach and practice authentic evangelism, I am always on the lookout for resources that are at once richly theological and uncompromisingly practical. Mark Teasdale's *Evangelism for Non-Evangelists* is such a book. It rescues evangelism from surface methods and dehumanizing formulas as it helps the faithful to navigate the waters of genuine gospel encounter."

Al Tizon, affiliate associate professor of missional and global leadership, North Park Theological Seminary, executive minister, Serve Globally, Evangelical Covenant Church

"*Evangelism for Non-Evangelists* stands apart from other texts offering best practices and programs of evangelism. Mark Teasdale unpacks some of the negative baggage associated with evangelism and challenges the reader to reflect deeply on their beliefs and evaluate whether their evangelistic practices authentically flow out of their understanding of who God is and what God is doing in the world. This is a must-read for seminary students, pastors and lay leaders as they seek to share and embody the gospel in their communities and throughout the entire ministry of the local church."

Heather Heinzman Lear, director of evangelism ministries, The United Methodist Church

"Mark Teasdale navigates the topic of evangelism in a way that includes a wide variety of theological perspectives. His approach helps many persons find an authentic way of living out 'a bias for the good news.' This is a very helpful book for all who want a deeper and more practical approach to evangelism."

Scott J. Jones, former McCreless Associate Professor of Evangelism, Perkins School of Theology, Southern Methodist University

Evangelism for *Non*-Evangelists

Sharing the Gospel Authentically

MARK R. TEASDALE

IVP Academic

An imprint of InterVarsity Press
Downers Grove, Illinois

InterVarsity Press
P.O. Box 1400, Downers Grove, IL 60515-1426
ivpress.com
email@ivpress.com

InterVarsity Press® is the book-publishing division of InterVarsity Christian Fellowship/USA®, a movement of students and faculty active on campus at hundreds of universities, colleges and schools of nursing in the United States of America, and a member movement of the International Fellowship of Evangelical Students. For information about local and regional activities, visit intervarsity.org.

Scripture quotations, unless otherwise noted, are from the New Revised Standard Version of the Bible, copyright 1989 by the Division of Christian Education of the National Council of the Churches of Christ in the USA. Used by permission. All rights reserved.

While any stories in this book are true, some names and identifying information may have been changed to protect the privacy of individuals.

Cover design: Cindy Kiple
Interior design: Dan van Loon
Images: Deposit Photos/Glow Images

ISBN 978-0-8308-5166-9 (print)
ISBN 978-0-8308-8224-3 (digital)

Printed in the United States of America ♾

Library of Congress Cataloging-in-Publication Data

A catalog record for this book is available from the Library of Congress.

P	23	22	21	20	19	18	17	16	15	14	13	12	11	10	9	8	7	6	5	4	3	2	1
Y	36	35	34	33	32	31	30	29	28	27	26	25	24	23	22	21	20	19	18	17	16		

To Ana, Katarina and Luke,

who all have been good news in my life.

Contents

Acknowledgments

*I*n many ways I have been nurtured specifically for teaching evangelism thanks to the remarkable people God has placed in my life at critical junctions. Most influential was Dr. James Cecil Logan, the late E. Stanley Jones Professor of Evangelism at Wesley Theological Seminary in Washington, DC. Jim was a mentor and friend whom I first met while studying for my master of divinity. It was his guidance and example, along with the well-timed connections he made for me, that led me to pursue the study of evangelism as a lifelong calling.

Jim introduced me to the Foundation for Evangelism (FFE), which generously supported my PhD studies in evangelism with its Harry S. Denman Fellowship and has continued to support me through the E. Stanley Jones Professorship in Evangelism. I extend my thanks to the FFE and, in particular, to Paul Ervin and Jane Wood, who had a vision for equipping a new generation of evangelism scholars and worked tirelessly to build the infrastructure, raise the funds and forge the relationships necessary to make that vision a reality.

Along the way I received encouragement from a number of professors of evangelism who first served as my teachers and then graciously welcomed me into their ranks as a colleague. While there are too many of these to mention, I especially give thanks for William (Billy) Abraham and Elaine Heath, both of whom sat on my dissertation committee at Southern Methodist University, and Laceye Warner of Duke Divinity School, who has always provided me with invaluable advice.

For this book particularly I am indebted to Dr. Rick Richardson of Wheaton College, who was a source of affirmation in my work to build bridges between the mainline and evangelical branches of the church, and Dr. George Hunsberger, who selflessly dedicated his first weeks of retirement to reading and providing me feedback on the manuscript. Dr. Dan Reid, my editor at IVP, has also been tremendously helpful, often figuring out what I wanted to say and finding ways to express it better than I could. His editing and insight have been invaluable.

Introduction

*T*his past year I had conversations about religion with several people. These individuals included a humanist who leads worship in an Episcopalian congregation; a person who grew up in the church, is married to a pagan of the same sex and has begun questioning his own Christian beliefs; a pantheist who is married to an atheist; a member of a liberal mainline Protestant denomination who is in full agreement with the progressive political and theological agendas brought forward in that denomination; and a self-described evangelical who is struggling to find a place as a church planter within a mainline denomination that has been marked more by institutional upkeep than creative outreach. Perhaps it is not surprising that a professor of evangelism would carry on conversations about faith with such a variegated group of people. It may be more surprising to learn what these people shared in common: they were all students in seminary seeking degrees that would give them the academic credentials to be professional leaders in the church. This is the reality of teaching in a mainline denominational seminary today.

These students also had another point in common: they did not want to take my evangelism course. Many of my students find my class to be one of the least palatable aspects of moving through the seminary's curriculum. However, because of ordination and graduation requirements, they swallowed hard and registered.

Along these same lines, a good friend of mine who is the director of evangelism in a major Protestant denomination was telling me about a training session she had held for clergy and lay church leaders. Even though the word "evangelism" is in her title and she was invited to lead this session, she had debated whether to use the word "evangelism" in her presentation.

She was concerned that too many people would find the term off-putting and it would get in the way of her teaching.

If you are a seminary student taking an evangelism course or church leader tasked with developing an evangelism strategy for your church, perhaps you can relate to these experiences. You have entered into this endeavor with a sense of foreboding and uncertainty about what comes next. Visions of being accosted by aggressive people passing out tracts on the street corner, awkward silences as the pastor waits for someone to come forward during an altar call, folks knocking on doors to share their beliefs and literature—all done in the name of Jesus—may well be swimming through your head.

Or perhaps you have had positive experiences with evangelism and are braced to have your personal beliefs deconstructed. You are worried that the professor and your fellow students or church members will sneer at the charismatic experience you had under a faith healer or while attending the rally of a televangelist. Maybe you struggle with the fact that you are one of the people knocking on doors, leading altar calls or handing out tracts and that you do these things precisely because you love Jesus and want others to know the mighty gift of salvation he offers.

If you are teaching about evangelism, you know you have specific material to cover. There are certain theories and practices you have determined are essential for students to know. At the same time you recognize that you must address the potent emotional responses students experience. You are both the ticket agent providing what is necessary to progress to the next stop in ministry preparation and the porter who must help students check the often considerable amount of baggage they have brought along for the trip.

This book is written with all of you in mind. As a student who had to take the course in evangelism to receive his MDiv and now as a professor who teaches that course in a seminary, I understand the concerns brought to the table by those in both roles. I have suffered through the social awkwardness and sometimes offensiveness of poorly done evangelism. I have also knocked on doors, shared my faith on street corners and invited friends to pray the sinner's prayer. I appreciate the voices of those who come to the course with both positive and negative experiences of evangelism.

It is because I have experienced evangelism in all these ways—as learner, as teacher, as practitioner, as practiced upon, as grateful recipient and as uncomfortable resister—that I have written this book. Evangelism is a subject that cannot be studied apart from the experiences people bring to it. And each person's experience of evangelism is legitimate. To ignore our experiences as we enter the study of evangelism is to miss a key ingredient we need to learn the subject well. We cannot practice evangelism without putting our whole selves into it. To do this would be to commit one of the worst mistakes possible in the understanding and practice of evangelism: to be inauthentic.

We all know what it feels like when someone is trying too hard to win our approval. If the person is offering something worthwhile, it will be evident in how they relate to us. If the person constantly seeks to cover up their true self to make what they are offering seem more appealing, that is disconcerting. Most of us can smell a phony a mile away, and we take off once we catch a whiff. This is the same for individuals and for entire organizations. No one wants to join an organization that has a great façade but no substance on the inside.

The same is true in evangelism. Only when we offer the good news of Jesus Christ as that which has touched and transformed our lives does it become meaningful and interesting to others. Only when we are authentic to who we are in Christ is evangelism done well.

We can do our best to practice evangelism by learning the so-called best practices propounded by evangelism gurus. A great many local churches have taken this route—putting up good signage in buildings, maintaining sufficient parking, making sure attendees are greeted, cleaning the restrooms until sparkling, and creating fun and welcoming children's areas. However, these strategies do not guarantee meaningful evangelism. A church—or individual—can perfect all these practices and still come across as inauthentic, even creepy. This is because the practices are shallow if they do not convey who we are and how we came to our beliefs in the good news.

I am not against excellence in our practice of evangelism. To the contrary, I think a great many Christians, local churches and even denominations do not take seriously that "we are therefore Christ's ambassadors, as though God were making his appeal through us" (2 Cor 5:20 NIV). As God's representatives we ought to put forward the best impression we can. However, the church's programming and facilities are often put to shame by the excellence found in the marketplace and political arena—and these are appealing for our dollars or votes rather than the redemption of the universe. We should do better than this!

Still, our programming and facilities should not be what recommends our message to others. Jesus said people would know we were his by our love, not by our remarkable youth programs or spacious buildings. It is when we share our genuine selves with people that the good news comes through most clearly and appealingly.

In this book I take as my premise the need to approach evangelism authentically. This means I leave room for people of differing theologies and in different places in their faith journey to engage with evangelism. My goal is not to convince you to adopt a specific way of understanding or practicing evangelism (though I certainly have my own ideas about this) but to provide you with the tools to think through evangelism for yourself.

The overriding metaphor I use throughout the book to explain the process of developing authentic evangelism is that of navigation. Working with evangelism is a multistep process that requires preparation and guidance if we are to arrive safely at the intended destination. At times navigation requires us to avoid dangers lurking on the journey. At other times it requires us to pause and reflect on where we have been and where we want to go so we can chart the next leg of the voyage. In the end our hope is to arrive at an authentic understanding and practice of evangelism. This will allow us to share a message that we firmly believe is so good it is worth sharing.

This book is not a map for how to arrive at this destination. Rather, it is a guide for how to spot the difficulties ahead, how to gain a general sense of direction for the trip and how to recognize what will be useful along the way. This process is not an easy one. If you persevere, though, what you generate from the undertaking will be uniquely yours—yours to share with others.

A Disclaimer: Evangelism as a Bias

In order to navigate successfully to an authentic practice of evangelism, we need to start with clarity about what we mean by "evangelism." As William Abraham has observed, evangelism is both descriptive and normative.[1] This means that those who study and practice evangelism must make statements

---

[1]William J. Abraham, *The Logic of Evangelism* (Grand Rapids: Wm. B. Eerdmans, 1989), 11.

about how they believe the world ought to operate as well as describe the way it actually operates now. Following this insight, let me share my own definition of evangelism: Evangelism is a bias for the good news.

This is a provocative definition for three reasons. First, it uses the word "bias," which is almost never construed as a positive thing. In the case of evangelism it raises the specter of all the judgmental evangelists who make us uneasy. "Evangelism" is a word that ends with the suffix "–ism," though, and just like any other word that ends in "–ism," it denotes a bias in favor of one thing and against another thing. Most "isms," including racism, sexism and nativism, argue for one group of people over and against another group of people—one race, sex or ethnicity is preferred over all others. If evangelism is a similar "ism," we had best stop now before we multiply further the sins of the world.

However, evangelism is not like these other "isms." Rather than promoting one group of people over another, it declares one message over all other messages. It declares that there is supremacy to "good news," and it rejects all other forms of news as deficient.

This brings us to the second provocative aspect of the definition. It does not assert what this good news is. This is by design. It allows space for Christians from a variety of theological traditions to approach evangelism.[2] Each of us must work through our beliefs about God to determine what we hold to be the central good news of the Christian faith, and no Christian theological tradition is disbarred from this process.

Christians have long claimed that there is a central message about God's goodness, often referred to as the "gospel" (which literally means "good news"). An enormous amount has been written about what the gospel is, much of it posted on blogs. Most of these agree that the gospel at least deals with God's good nature, the human need for God's goodness and God reaching out through Jesus Christ to invite people into God's goodness.

While it is up to each of us to navigate through these ideas about God's nature and human need so we can construct our own articulation of the

---

[2]By "theological traditions," I mean any organized understanding of the Christian faith (e.g., evangelicalism, Pentecostalism, liberation theology, process theology). I use this term in place of the more common "theologies" to make a clear demarcation between the practice of theological reflection we engage in and the preexisting fruits of that reflection we use to inform our beliefs. We will discuss this later on in the book.

gospel, the insights of N. T. Wright are helpful here. First, he reminds us that "the Christian message is about good news, not good advice." He explains that this good news does more than just prod us to consider going to heaven instead of going to hell. Rather, it "affects everything: how we understand our relationship to God, the future, our responsibilities as a church and as disciples, and much more."[3]

Wright goes on to suggest that any formulation of the gospel must include three elements: something has happened, something will happen and we are now living in a time between what did happen and what will happen. This was the pattern of what Jesus announced in reference to the coming of the kingdom of God (the kingdom has come; the kingdom will be consummated by the Son of Man; repent in preparation for its fulfillment) and of what the disciples announced about Jesus (the Son of God was incarnate, crucified and resurrected in the person of Jesus of Nazareth; Jesus will come again in glory; repent and enter the community of the church).[4]

My own view of the good news accepts the incarnation, death and bodily resurrection of the Lord Jesus Christ and looks forward to Jesus returning to establish the kingdom of God in glory. Until then, I believe that God is redeeming the world through Jesus Christ in the power of the Holy Spirit and that we are invited to participate in that redemption process. I write this not to convince you that this is the only way to articulate the good news but so that you understand where I am coming from in this text.

One reason I articulate the good news this way is that it makes one point very clear: Evangelism does not reject any person. What it rejects are messages and powers that would deny people the ability to share in God's gracious redemption through Jesus Christ. Evangelism denounces whatever stands between people and God's redeeming work, even if it is the church or Christians that form this hindrance.

This view of the gospel also proscribes any action that is angry or condemning from being evangelism. People who pass judgment on other people in the name of Jesus are not doing evangelism. They may be making a

---

[3]N. T. Wright, *Simply Good News: Why the Gospel Is News and What Makes It Good* (New York: HarperOne, 2015), 5.
[4]Ibid., 17.

statement about their faith, but they are not grounding that statement in good news. Rather, they are hindering people from hearing the good news by stating that, for whatever reason, various people are not capable of entering God's redemptive work through Jesus Christ. This is the opposite of evangelism. It navigates any attempt at evangelism right off a cliff.

Whatever your definition of "good news" may be, construct it in such a way that no person is on the negative end of the bias it entails. Evangelism should reject that which is harmful and hurtful to people but never people themselves. This is not to suggest that evangelism will always be easy for people to hear or accept. The bias we articulate about what God is doing may well conflict with an existing set of beliefs that a person holds. This, however, is not a rejection of the person.

The third reason this definition of evangelism is provocative is that it does not reduce evangelism to a specific set of activities. There are two perspectives on what practices fall under the rubric of evangelism. Some scholars state that evangelism includes only those practices that involve inviting people to receive the good news of God. Others claim that evangelism entails both the invitation and, for those who have accepted the invitation, practices of formation that shape people as Christians. With this definition, I declare my membership in the latter group.

A bias is not just an opinion or an intellectual position but a claim that shapes those who hold it. Consider this: A capitalist is not someone who holds a specific view on how to engage in economic activity but who can just as easily participate in communist activities while disagreeing intellectually. No, a capitalist is someone who has been formed into a series of beliefs about how to value goods, labor and services. For a capitalist to take part in a communist system would require either coercion or conversion to overcome how the person was formed as a capitalist. Likewise, to define evangelism as a bias means that those who accept the good news must be formed by the good news. In addition, since the good news points to the eternally good God, this formation never has an end. Even those who have long been adherents of the good news can continue to be evangelized.

If evangelism is a bias, it demands that we who study and practice it be intentional and discerning in our tasks. Biases that have been deployed for evil have caused deep pain in this world. We do not want to add to this pain either on purpose or by our carelessness in allowing evangelism to be used as a weapon against others. The work we are about to embark on requires our full attention.

Tools for Thinking Authentically About Evangelism

There are four areas we need to move through to navigate evangelism. First is articulating our starting point, which is our core belief in the goodness of God that motivates us to evangelize. Second is theologically reflecting on our starting point. Third is becoming contextually aware. Fourth is developing creative practices as the concrete manifestation of the good news. Doing all of this requires us to steer through a complex course of beliefs, traditions and cultural forces to arrive at our destination of an authentic understanding and practice of evangelism.

It is important to recognize that none of these four areas is inconsequential. All are interconnected and all are necessary. If an evangelist, anxious to save souls, jumps straight to telling people about Jesus without first reflecting on why she believes what she does, she may well run into serious problems when her listeners challenge those beliefs. Likewise, if a church committee spends hours perfecting a statement of the church's theology but focuses only on maintaining the church's institutional structure with no concern for the community, it has failed to practice evangelism. Neither of these entities has navigated through the full route of evangelism. Both have foundered before reaching the destination of engaging in authentic evangelistic practice.

The following formula provides an alternative way of understanding how the four parts relate to one another:

$$\text{Starting Point} + \text{Theological Reflection} + \text{Contextual Awareness} = \frac{\text{Creative}}{\text{Practice}}$$

In this formula, when the starting point is summed together with theological reflection and contextual awareness, it creates the capacity for us to develop creative evangelistic practices. The whole of the equation—starting point, theological reflection, contextual awareness and creative practice—is how we navigate evangelism. We will spend most of this book discussing the four parts of navigating evangelism and how they interact with each other.

IMPLICATIONS

There are several implications to approaching the study of evangelism this way. The first and most important is that it makes evangelism accessible and practicable for a variety of people, regardless of their theological traditions. Although evangelism is often associated with evangelical, fundamentalist and Pentecostal traditions, navigating evangelism in the way I suggest allows for people from any theological tradition to engage in it.

Opening the door for various theological traditions also opens the door for people within those traditions to recast their favored practices as evangelistic. For example, the liberation theologian can point to living in community with the poor as an authentic way of practicing the good news,[5] just as the Pentecostal can point to a ministry of deliverance from evil spirits and the evangelical can point to developing neighborhood Bible studies as authentic evangelistic practices.

This widens the scope of evangelism and makes it a bridge-building practice rather than a divisive one.[6] This bridge building occurs first within the church. Those of us who hold to different theological traditions can stop avoiding one another or seeing each other as working counter to the true purposes of God—this model of evangelism allows us to better understand the hopes, beliefs and practices of our brothers and sisters in Christ.

My hope is that this realization will lead us to stop seeing our particular brands of evangelism as the only way for others to experience the redemptive work of God through Jesus Christ. Instead we will see our work as complemented by the work of other Christians who approach evangelism differently. The Pentecostal, for example, can value the demand for systemic justice brought by the liberationist while the liberationist can value how the Pentecostal trusts the power of the Holy Spirit to transform lives and cultures. Far from making us withdraw from one another out of concern that we will either be offended or cause offense, evangelism becomes an opportunity for us to share our deepest beliefs with one another frankly and respectfully.

---

[5]Priscilla Pope-Levison provides insightful analysis on the intersection of evangelism and liberation theology in *Evangelization from a Liberation Perspective* (New York: Peter Lang, 1991), 159.

[6]The Academy for Evangelism in Theological Education dedicated its 2013 meeting to this theme of evangelism as bridge building. Some of the presentations offered at this meeting can be found in *Witness: The Journal of the Academy for Evangelism in Theological Education* 28 (2014).

This internal rapprochement paves the way for us to build bridges between those who claim the good news of Jesus Christ and those who do not. If Christians value the different ways those within the church practice evangelism, would not the church provide a richer witness to the good news of God? Those outside the church could observe Christians who love one another and who love the world by engaging in a wide variety of activities demonstrating that love.

Outside of these larger effects, navigating evangelism also helps us make sense of the proliferation of evangelism material, both scholarly and popular. From books to tracts to Internet videos to denominational resources and kits, there is no lack of material on offer. It can be difficult to get a handle on these resources because despite using the same terminology they tend to define terms differently and employ different methodologies.[7] The navigation model offers a quick way to grasp core ideas. What is the great hope that motivates the authors as their starting point? What theological traditions do the authors espouse? By answering these questions we can get to the heart of what the author thinks about evangelism. We can also determine whether the practices of evangelism on offer fit what is authentic to us.

Making this determination has practical value. Any number of struggling local congregations can gesture toward a pile of expensive evangelism materials they have purchased and followed over the years, to very little effect. The chief reason for this is not that there were flaws in the materials but that the activities presented were not authentic demonstrations of what the congregations believed. The inauthenticity of the practices doomed the effort from the start and left the congregation feeling even more despondent.

Likewise, congregations and pastors can use the navigation process to understand each other better. Navigating evangelism provides the basic outline for helping clergy and laity to recognize each other's hopes, theology and practices so they can find ways to work more effectively together to share the good news.

---

[7]I explored this idea in an article surveying evangelism texts published by United Methodist authors. In spite of their common denominational background, I found that they all employed different definitions of the word "evangelism," different methodologies for studying evangelism and different examples of the best practitioners of evangelism. Mark R. Teasdale, "The Contribution to Missiology by United Methodist Scholarship on Evangelism," *Missiology* 41, no. 4 (2013): 452-61.

More than understanding each other, navigating evangelism offers a way for those of us who are Christians to create our own authentic ways of practicing evangelism. This pushes back against cookie cutter models suggesting that all Christians or congregations must act or believe the same way to engage in evangelism effectively. To be authentic about the good news of God's redemption through Jesus Christ in the power of the Holy Spirit is to be effective. This approach to evangelism advocates for evangelism that is sensitive to the time and place where it is practiced and authentic to the beliefs of the Christians practicing it.

Ending the cookie cutter approach to evangelism has two other benefits. First, it helps atone for the church's past sins. That evangelism has been the site of painful encounters between the church and those it sought to incorporate into the Christian faith is undeniable. Books such as Luis Rivera's *Violent Evangelism*, which traces the evangelistic practices involved in the Spanish conquest of the New World, remind us that Christians have used the propagation of the good news as a cover for avarice and pride.[8] A model of evangelism that allows us to navigate our beliefs while remaining contextually sensitive demonstrates that Christians do not accept these past misdeeds. We believe in good news that is good both for the evangelist and for those hearing it for the first time.

Second, it differentiates evangelism from the slough of strong opinions found in our age of social media. We are awash in Twitter feeds, comment sections, blogs, reviewer apps and countless other means for sharing our opinions. We may be hesitant to evangelize, but a large number of people in the early twenty-first century are comfortable stating their beliefs on a great many subjects with little or no attempt to filter their thoughts, much less consider alternative perspectives or the ways their beliefs might be offensive to others.[9]

By navigating evangelism, we equip ourselves to eschew this kind of boorish behavior. Evangelism becomes more than just sharing our opinion; the way we share the good news becomes an embodiment of the good news.

---

[8]Luis N. Rivera, *A Violent Evangelism: The Political and Religious Conquest of the Americas* (Louisville, KY: Westminster John Knox, 1992).

[9]Os Guinness, *The Global Public Square: Religious Freedom and the Making of a World Safe for Diversity* (Downers Grove, IL: InterVarsity Press, 2013), 56.

This means we communicate in ways that are civil and considerate of others' dignity while remaining grounded in our unwavering experience of God's goodness in our own lives. Such communication is welcoming rather than condemning and invites others to consider our message rather than react with further diatribe. To Wright's point, it demonstrates that we have good news to share of an actual transformation God has made in the world and in our lives. It is not just good advice that comes from our own strongly held beliefs without any grounding in God's action.

Under the best of circumstances, evangelism is a contentious activity. Jesus was clear about this in his instructions to the disciples in Matthew 10. If we learn to navigate evangelism, at least we will be able to avoid the pitfalls that have hampered the evangelistic work of the church in the past and that diminishes the value of human thought today. At best we will offer a welcome message of hope that will be a blessing to those who hear us.

Chapter One

Evangelists Are
Taught, Not Born

*A*teenage boy stood in an open, trash-littered lot by a rundown liquor store. It was twilight, and the waning sun made it hard to see, though it was clear that the liquor store was doing a brisk business. Most of the patrons held their purchases in brown paper bags that they quickly inverted into their mouths as they exited the store.

The boy was not alone. He was part of a group of about twenty other teenagers who had arrived in the lot late in the afternoon. Equipped with small pamphlets explaining the gospel message through various cartoons and illustrations, the boy prayed with his colaborers, listened to the musical group that had been appointed to attract people's attention, then awaited an opportunity to share the great salvation available through Jesus Christ.

He was not idle long. Several people came to listen to the music and turned to engage in conversation with the teenagers, including one man who struck up a conversation with the boy. This was exciting for everyone in the group—it was exactly what they had hoped would take place.

Then, something unexpected happened. This boy, who had been raised in the church, who in first grade had prayed to receive Jesus Christ as his Lord and Savior, who had even preached the Sunday morning service at fifteen years old and who was admired as a paragon of teenage faith within the group, froze. He was petrified with fear. He did not know what to say or how to proceed as he faced the amiable person who had begun speaking with him.

The level of shame the boy felt was immense. It was heightened when one of the younger members of the group who was known for his immaturity recognized the boy's distress and came to pick up the conversation where the boy had faltered. Crushed, the boy hid in the back of the group for the rest of the evening. When the group gathered for a final prayer that night, he broke down in tears as he confessed before God and his peers his failure as an evangelist.

Almost twenty-five years later, this same boy sat down to write the book you are now reading, believing with all his heart that evangelists are made, not born.

OVERCOMING STEREOTYPES

As we begin navigating evangelism we need to jettison unhelpful or dangerous ideas that threaten to bring us to a halt or sink us entirely before we even have a chance to talk to another person about our faith. The best way to do this is by expanding our view of evangelism beyond the associations we have with it.

We all have a tendency to reduce people, ideas and situations to the easiest set of concepts available to us. This allows us to avoid nuance and the uncomfortable realization that people, things and events are rarely as simple as we would like to believe. Often this reductionism is negative, reducing whatever is within our sight to its most unflattering depiction.

There is a reason we slip into reductionism. It makes life easier. We can quickly categorize whatever we encounter as good, bad or indifferent. We can assess how much of our time and energy we believe it is worth and then move on to the next thing, having convinced ourselves that we have dealt with it fully and appropriately.

But the speed and assurance of reductionism comes at a cost. In exchange for the convenience of easy categorization, we reduce people to two-dimensional figures, nuanced ideas into sound bites and complex situations into zero-sum competitions in which a winner must emerge.

Evangelism, perhaps more than most ideas, suffers from reductionism. Sadly, much of this reductionism is negative and comes as a direct result of our personal experiences. Moving beyond the stereotypes that come from this reductionism is essential if we are to move ahead in our navigation. Two of the most common stereotypes are of the kind of person who does evangelism—the evangelist—and the theology we associate with evangelism—evangelicalism.

EVANGELISTS

Evangelists are people we usually see as unswervingly committed to their faith and persistent in sharing it. We also may see them as flawed or even sinister. Sinclair Lewis, an early twentieth-century American author, summed up this stereotype in his description of the title character of his novel *Elmer Gantry*, who becomes an evangelist of national renown:

> A huge young man, Elmer Gantry; six foot one, thick, broad, big handed; a large face, handsome as a Great Dane is handsome, and a swirl of black hair, worn rather long. His eyes were friendly, his smile was friendly—oh, he was always friendly enough; he was merely astonished when he found that you did not understand his importance and did not want to hand over anything he might desire. He was a baritone solo turned into portly flesh; he was a gladiator laughing at the comic distortion of his wounded opponent.[1]

As this description hints at, there is a tendency for us to imagine evangelists as larger than life. The term conjures images of famous Christian preachers and apostles such as Billy Graham, D. L. Moody, Charles Finney, John Wesley and even St. Paul. These individuals all seem peculiarly gifted for evangelism. They were not regular people who happened into great evangelistic work but great evangelists who lived into their natural greatness. Even the evangelists we believe have done harm still often seem like giants in their own way.

Regardless of whether we perceive a specific evangelist as coercive, duplicitous, gentle or loving, we often reduce that evangelist to the epitome of the preconceptions we have in mind. The evangelist has either performed superhuman acts of good in sharing the gospel or engaged in monstrous evil by deceiving others.

The Bible lends credence to the perception that evangelists are set aside from regular humanity. In Ephesians 4:11, evangelists are listed alongside apostles, prophets, pastors and teachers as those who have received a special gift from God to help strengthen the body of Christ. The only person specifically told to do "the work of an evangelist" is Paul's protégé Timothy in 2 Timothy 4:5. This would seem to be rarefied company indeed.

Yet while the Bible acknowledges that God calls some people to be evangelists, it is also clear that God commands and equips all followers of Jesus

---

[1]Sinclair Lewis, *Elmer Gantry* (New York: Dell, 1927), 13.

Christ to undertake evangelistic work. This is evident in the Great Commission, Jesus' farewell speech to his followers given as he completed his
earthly ministry following his resurrection. While Jesus addressed these
words, recorded at the end of Matthew 28, to his apostles, the Gospel writer
indicates that he was including those still doubtful about the resurrection.
In doing this Jesus made it clear that all who followed him were called and
equipped to do the work of evangelism, not just those with unshakable faith.
This holds true for the apostles who first heard Jesus and for those of us who
read the Great Commission today.

Jesus' command in the Great Commission to go into all the world and
make disciples reinforces the universality of the call to evangelism. There
are no requirements to meet before we go, there is just the imperative that
we do go. Lest we feel out of our depth in this endeavor, Jesus accompanies
this command with the promise of God's provision. After describing himself
as the one who holds all authority in heaven and on earth, he states that he
will be with us always, even to the end of the age. Here is the power of God to
make disciples given to all God's followers.

What is remarkable about this promise is not that it grants Christians
superpowers by allowing them to tap into the cosmic authority of Christ. It's
better than that! It explains the nature of the world in which Christians will
share their faith. When Christians engage in evangelism, they do so with
"home field advantage," knowing Jesus' presence and power are already at
work ministering God's good news to those with whom they interact. This
makes possible Jesus' command to "go

LEARNING ACTIVITY

The New Testament records
five commissioning passages
between Jesus and the
disciples, not just one. These
are Matthew 28:16-20,
Mark 16:9-20, Luke 24:36-53,
John 20:19-31 and Acts 1:1-11.
Break into five groups, with
each group looking at one of
these passages. Answer three
questions in reference to each
passage: (1) What commands
does Jesus give? (2) What
promises does Jesus make?
(3) What is the hoped-for
outcome of following Jesus'
commands? In doing this, we
often find that evangelism is
much more multifaceted than
we first imagined.

into all the world" to make disciples, since the entire world and its inhabitants are already touched by the resurrection.

When we look at it from this perspective, our concerns about evangelists being a "different breed" evaporate. While there will always be gifted evangelists who seem larger than life, the work of evangelism is not meant solely for these select few. According to Jesus in the Great Commission, an evangelist is a common person who seeks to live into the promise that the risen Christ is with all people.

EVANGELISM ≠ EVANGELICALISM

Along with their stereotypical view of evangelists, many people reduce evangelism by equating it with evangelicalism. I have run across numerous people (even other theology professors!) who use these terms interchangeably. They are not the same thing. Evangelism is the practice of sharing the good news. Evangelicalism is a specific tradition within the Christian faith. Since the late twentieth century, the term "evangelical" has also been linked to conservative political ideas. These political connotations are not traditionally part of evangelicalism, nor do all self-described evangelicals accept them.

There is historical precedent for conflating evangelicalism and evangelism. During the eighteenth and nineteenth centuries, a variety of revival movements swept through Europe and North America encouraging people to go deeper in their faith. In doing this, they demonstrated the four attributes that have come to be associated with classical evangelicalism: (1) biblicism, (2) crucicentrism, (3) conversionism and (4) activism.[2] Biblicism refers to the high level of authority that evangelicals grant to the Bible, receiving the written text as at least sufficient to teach the way of salvation. Crucicentrism points to the evangelical focus on the death and atonement of Christ as of central importance in Christian theology. Conversionism and activism point to the evangelical insistence on enacting faith, the former by inviting people to become Christians, the latter by demonstrating the gospel through efforts to improve people's lives both individually and corporately.

Evangelicals are also known for their pietism.[3] This means they value a heart-based religion in which people feel the assurance of God's acceptance

---

[2]David Bebbington, *Evangelicalism in Modern Britain: A History from the 1730s to the 1980s* (London: Unwin Hyman, 1989), 3.
[3]Ibid., 39-40.

and love. When pietism is combined with the four attributes of classical evangelicalism, it is easy to see why evangelicals hold evangelism closely. Evangelicalism as a theological tradition values heartfelt responses to the message of Jesus Christ as related to the Bible. It is also a tradition that calls people to undergo a decisive conversion so they can live according to the will of God.

Evangelicals have engaged in powerful evangelism throughout history. Examples of this are the Wesleyan Revival in Great Britain, the Great Awakenings in the United States and the expansive missionary movements launched from Europe and the United States during the nineteenth century. Within these nation-spanning movements, specific practices were developed that became synonymous with evangelism. These included preaching, praying and singing hymns that invited people to confess their sins, accept Jesus Christ as their Lord and Savior and feel the assurance of God's forgiveness.[4]

Even though the cultures in the United States shifted away from supporting evangelicalism during the twentieth century, evangelical evangelism has continued unabated.[5] Drawing together large crowds for the purpose of sharing the gospel and calling people to conversion remains an accepted practice. Adapting to new ways of gathering, these crowds can be gathered via radio, television, the Internet, mobile app or whatever the current technology allows.

Evangelical evangelism is perhaps most visible in how it continues to influence the practice of evangelism today. Imagine this scenario: It's a warm night, but you and several of your friends are huddled close to a large bonfire. You have just finished singing several songs that both excite and lull your senses. You are tired and happy at the end of a long week. A camp counselor stands in the midst of the group and invites you to give your life to Christ so you can share in this kind of fellowship eternally. Now, shift the image. You are sitting in a large auditorium. A band consisting of people playing guitars, keyboards and drums, along with several vocalists, has finished playing thirty minutes of high-energy songs interspersed with prayers that God would

---

[4]Robert G. Tuttle, *The Story of Evangelism: A History of the Witness to the Gospel* (Nashville: Abingdon, 2006), 337-39; Leigh Eric Schmidt, *Holy Fairs: Scotland and the Making of American Revivalism*, 2nd ed. (Grand Rapids: Eerdmans, 2001), xi-xxix.

[5]Sydney Ahlstrom, *A Religious History of the American People*, 2nd ed. (New Haven, CT: Yale University Press, 2004), 956-57.

meet people in the midst of the music. The preacher walks onto the stage and reminds you that God can forgive your sins if you will accept Christ.

Even more theologically liberal congregations tend to assume that these evangelical practices are the only way to engage in evangelism. This assumption leads to a theological disconnect between the people practicing evangelism and the practices they use. The discomfort that comes from trying to force a progressive theologian into an evangelical mold is a primary reason that Christians in mainline denominations often choose to hide the practice of evangelism under their ecclesiastical beds. They believe that to take evangelism seriously means to become evangelical, and this is something they do not want to do.

If those of us studying evangelism are to be effective in moving past this reduction of evangelism to evangelicalism, it is critical for us to recognize that evangelism is available for anyone who is a Christian. Regardless of where we stand theologically, we can just as fully articulate our view of the Christian faith and just as authentically practice evangelism as any other Christian. The good news of Jesus Christ is not known and articulated only through the evangelical tradition. There is no Christian theology that has a unique claim on evangelism.

LEARNING ACTIVITY

When studying evangelism, it is important that we expand our knowledge of different theological traditions. Often we hold stereotyped views of each tradition (e.g., liberationists care only about politics, fundamentalists care only about saving souls). Gaining a clearer picture of the variety of theological traditions allows us to appreciate the nuances of each tradition and articulate our own beliefs.

MOVING PAST CULTURAL PRESSURE

It is not easy to expand our view of evangelism by moving past our reductionisms. We tend to cling to our stereotypes. However, it is necessary that we let go of the false security these bring. Freed from them we are better able to navigate toward claiming evangelism in an authentic way.

It will take us most of the book to unpack how we make this claim since it involves both our starting point and our theological reflection. In charting our way, we need to understand that claiming an authentic understanding and practice of evangelism requires us to make a normative claim.[6] This means that when we study and practice evangelism we must be ready to explain how we think things ought to be.

All theological fields of study require their adherents to make some sort of normative claim. Often these claims are made at the interpretive level, determining what data ought to be used to understand all other information within that field. When we study history, for example, we must determine which line of historiography we will use to interpret the past. In biblical studies we must determine what hermeneutic we will use to read the scriptural text. In theology we must determine which methodology to deploy in reflecting on the beliefs of the Christian faith. In this regard, evangelism follows the same pattern.

However, evangelism is different in two ways. First, it requires us to make a meta-level claim. This means we are not making a claim that has meaning only within the study of evangelism but a claim that stretches across academic fields and even into daily life.[7] Second, evangelism invites others to accept the same normative claim we are making. A historian, biblical scholar or theologian may develop a highly controversial view in his or her academic field but never have to share it beyond those within that field. As evangelists we are called not only to make a normative claim about how the world should be but also to share that claim with as many people as possible in the hope they will accept it.

The idea of making such a wide-ranging claim and then inviting people to share it is unsettling to say the least. In those parts of the world touched by the Enlightenment, this discomfort has much to do with the impact of modernity and postmodernity.[8] We must learn the contours of each of these if we are to navigate around the obstacles each presents to us.

---

[6]Abraham, *The Logic of Evangelism*, 11.

[7]See the appendix for a detailed explanation of how the study of evangelism influences other theological fields of study.

[8]Several texts address the influence of modernity and postmodernity on evangelism. Abraham, *The Logic of Evangelism*, and Bryan Stone, *Evangelism After Christendom: The Theology and Practice of Christian Witness* (Grand Rapids: Brazos, 2007), both include a section specifically on modernity. Brad J. Kallenberg, *Live to Tell: Evangelism for a Postmodern Age* (Grand Rapids: Brazos, 2002) deals with postmodernity and evangelism. Almost all evangelism books by Leonard Sweet approach evangelism from the vantage point of postmodernity.

MODERNITY

Modernity is best understood as the various impacts, especially intellectual and cultural, of the Enlightenment. During the Enlightenment people realized that they were not dependent on royal or ecclesiastical authorities to make sense of the world around them. Three major insights spurred this realization: (1) Truth exists and is absolute. (2) Absolute truth is universally applicable. (3) All people have access to this absolute truth through the use of their senses and reason.[9] As an illustration, consider the age-old picture of Sir Isaac Newton sitting under the apple tree. The truth is that gravity exists and will pull the apple from the tree toward the ground. This truth is absolute. It also holds true no matter where Sir Isaac Newton sits under an apple tree. Whether he is in Nepal, England or Antarctica, the apple will fall. Even if he sits under a tree on the moon, the apple will still have gravity work on it, although the lower mass of the moon makes the pull of gravity less on the apple. Finally, the truth that an apple will behave according to the force of gravity is something anyone can access by sensing the apple falling (by seeing it, hearing it bump the ground or feeling it hit them on the head).

These ideas so permeated common thought that they moved beyond the academic realm and generated a cultural modernity. One of the chief cultural results was the separation of the public and the private. That which could be demonstrated through the senses or reason was something suitable for public discussion. That which could not be proven with the senses or reason could still be believed by an individual or a group but was for their private enjoyment. It was not only bad manners to make these private ideas public, it was intellectually absurd. After all, why discuss publicly something that no one but the speaker could reasonably accept as true?

Religion fell into the category of the private. It was not disallowed, but it was to be practiced only by individuals or groups of like-minded individuals. While most countries under the influence of the Enlightenment forged compromises so religion would not be removed entirely from the public sphere (think of the words "In God We Trust" on the currency in the United States), it became largely taboo for people to engage in religious practice too overtly.

---

[9]I am indebted to Bruce Marshall, Lehman Professor of Christian Doctrine at Southern Methodist University, for helping me think through these three descriptors for modernity.

The impact on evangelism was predictably negative. A practice dedicated to sharing religious beliefs became less respectable as modernity found its way into the popular culture. Even at the height of the evangelical revivals in the eighteenth and nineteenth centuries, the influence of modernity was evident in how evangelists called people to personal salvation—salvation became a matter between the individual and God. Daily life was categorized away from one's notion of salvation, more defined by practical experience, expertise and engagement with the structures of commerce and politics. And as the revivals waned, evangelists became less welcome. Christian groups instead chose to pursue more publicly acceptable practices of their faith, such as establishing hospitals and orphanages.

These influences of modernity continue to hold sway in many Western churches, and they are significant impediments to people navigating toward their own understanding and practice of evangelism. Since evangelism is a matter of publicly sharing private beliefs that are not founded on data collected through the senses, engaging in it can make a person come across as an unreasonable lunatic. This is hardly a pleasant prospect. Even when Western Christians can articulate what they authentically believe, the heavy predisposition against public sharing of faith makes developing practices for sharing those beliefs unpalatable. It seems to commit what the Enlightenment defined as a cardinal sin: taking a step into the irrational.

As potent as the influence of modernity is, it is not the only cultural influence through which we must navigate. Where modernity has begun to lose its grip, postmodernity has taken its place. And while we might have expected that with the decline of modernity the disposition against evangelism would be removed, in fact it has gotten worse.

POSTMODERNITY

The word "postmodern" is often used as a blanket term to describe an array of intellectual, cultural and social shifts that have taken place from the mid-twentieth century to the present in the West.[10] Postmodernity's goal is to move past modernity by rejecting and reinterpreting the assumptions of the

---

[10]Lawrence Cahoone, ed., *From Modernism to Postmodernism: An Anthology*, 2nd ed. (Malden, MA: Blackwell Publishing, 2003), 221-23.

Enlightenment. We can see this by contrasting the basic assumptions of postmodernity with those of modernity.

First, instead of believing that truth is absolute, postmodernity argues that truth, while it may exist, is of secondary importance. In place of truth, narrative takes center stage. Rather than people seeking to discern the truth of the universe and to align with it, they seek to find a narrative that is meaningful to them. The extent to which a person's narrative fits with any empirically verifiable truth is irrelevant so long as the narrative grants the person a sense of meaning.

Second, since truth is irrelevant to meaning in a postmodern world, the issue is not that truth is universally applicable but that the universe is filled with a vast number of narratives from which to choose. This has the opposite effect of modernity. Whereas in modernity everyone is expected to abide by the absolute truth regardless of background or any other factor, in postmodernity pluralism and diversity are celebrated. All narratives are equally valuable because there is no overarching truth that serves as a litmus test for whether narratives are good or bad. The individual is the only one who can judge them, and then only on the basis of whether he or she finds the narrative to be meaningful.

Third, just as in modernity all people have access to the truth through their senses and reason, in postmodernity all people have the right to explore as many narratives as they wish until they feel fulfilled. They can explore individually or in groups. They can use existing narratives or create new ones. There are no taboos or strictures on this exploration; everything from sex to religion to politics to nature to pop culture is open for consideration.

So, to revisit our picture of Sir Isaac Newton, the issue is not that gravity made the apple fall on his head; it is how the apple tree came to be planted where he was sitting. Rather than arriving at a certainty that gravity would work regardless of where Newton was sitting, the goal would be for him to explore and experience different apple-related cultures, traditions and rituals of life in places where apple trees grow. And instead of penning a treatise on gravity to help people use their senses and reason to understand it, Newton might gather with a group of friends who could all seek to interact with a variety of flora and return to write stories about how humanity intertwines with nature. They would share their stories with each other, possibly helping one another adopt new narratives they had not encountered previously.

The shift to postmodernity initially looks like a good one for evangelism. The emphasis on narrative opens the door for people to be public about religion. We do not need to explain why we are religious. We just need to find our faith meaningful. And since all people are searching for meaningful narratives, evangelism could be seen as a means of offering one more option for consideration. However, postmodernity also brings two significant problems.

First, like modernity, postmodernity is centered on the individual. Modernity's premise is that all individuals can discover the absolute truths of the universe through their senses and reason. It grants the individual authority to determine whether the good news of God is in accordance with that truth. What seems rational to the individual trumps all else, allowing the individual to reject the good news out of hand.

While postmodernity is interested in meaningful narratives and not truth, its emphasis on the individual has the same effect on evangelism. If an individual does not find the good news meaningful, that person can reject it. Additionally, because both modernity and postmodernity understand people to be largely self-dependent and self-determining, sharing the good news about a redeeming God is difficult. The idea that an individual needs redemption from or for anything runs counter to our sense of sufficiency to determine what is truthful or meaningful within ourselves.

This brings us to the second problem. For all the openness of postmodernity, there is one great sin that can be committed against it: making a normative claim. To suggest that we have found a narrative that is superior to all other narratives in an absolute sense, not just in a sense that it is more meaningful for us personally, is anathema. Yet this is exactly what we as evangelists must do. As evangelists we state categorically that the good news of what God has done through Jesus Christ in the power of the Holy Spirit is the best possible narrative. It is the good news—the good news that defines the goodness of everything else. If other narratives move people away from this good news, we judge those narratives as mistaken. Likewise, if other narratives move people toward the good news, we judge them beneficial. Making such judgments runs against the postmodern ethic that all narratives have equal opportunity to prove themselves meaningful.

Evangelism does not fit within the assumptions of either modernity or postmodernity. Given that these are the two most significant definers of cultural values in the parts of the world influenced by the Enlightenment, there is enormous pressure against practicing evangelism in those regions. Evangelism is either irrational or judgmental. It either publicly airs what should be private or it refuses to accept the private individual's insistence on being able to explore any and all possible narratives publicly in a search for meaning. We must learn to navigate through these dangerous waters or we will founder in them, losing our nerve to share the good news with others.

FUNDAMENTALISM

Adding to this case against evangelism is the growing specter of fundamentalism. Fundamentalism originally developed in the early twentieth century in the United States as a Christian response to the influence of modernity. It drew its name from *The Fundamentals*. These articles urged readers to hold fast to core Christian beliefs, explaining why those beliefs were reasonable to accept even in the face of the intellectual challenges mounting against them.

Modernity was not kind to fundamentalism, and Western societies moved to stereotype those who accepted it rather than to engage with its intellectual claims. During much of the twentieth century in the United States, "fundamentalism" was a label that referred to a group of Christian conservatives who seemed to consign all those who disagreed with them to the wrath of God. To help people avoid this fate, fundamentalists shared their beliefs with others eagerly. However, most Americans did not receive this form of evangelism well because it was a zero-sum game—either one converted or was condemned. There was no middle ground.

This popular notion of fundamentalism has taken a sinister turn with the rise of extremism and radicalization in the early twenty-first century. Behavioral psychology describes the "fundamentalist mindset" as a dichotomizing and judgmental way of looking at the world. Such a mindset is not confined to any particular religion or even to conservatives.[11] Christians, Muslims, Buddhists or adherents of any other religion—or of no religion—can partake

---

[11]Charles B. Strozier, David M. Terman and James W. Jones, *The Fundamentalist Mindset* (New York: Oxford, 2010), xviii-xix, 7.

in a fundamentalist mindset regardless of whether they are conservative, liberal, progressive or anything else. Worse, many of these groups have demonstrated that their intolerance for other beliefs permits violence against those who disagree with them. Being associated with those who use physical coercion as a means to win converts can make us understandably skittish about claiming the role of evangelists.

Here it is important that we make a clear distinction. Condemning or harming those who disagree with us is wrong. It feeds into the worst kind of bigotry that evangelism can promote. It is hateful toward people and runs against what most religions teach. Rufus, the forgotten apostle from the sacrilegious but insightful movie *Dogma*, may have explained this best when he said, "[God] still digs humanity, but it bothers him to see the s——— that gets carried out in his name—wars, bigotry, televangelism. But especially the factioning of all the religions." Evangelism that builds walls or causes violence is something that Christians, along with people of all other religions and even no religion, can agree on as wrong. It is unworthy of the name "evangelism." We must steer well away from it.

Recognizing the evil that a fundamentalist mindset can bring about is not to say that it is wrong to have fundamental beliefs, however. Whether we articulate them or not, all of us have certain beliefs that we hold to be irreducibly right or wrong (as one of my professors used to say, nobody will question you if you state baldly that you believe it is wrong to roast babies on a spit at midnight for food). Having these sorts of absolute beliefs is not to be a fundamentalist; it is to be a well-functioning human being. And as evangelists we should recognize and articulate these beliefs. It is when we shut down conversation with others and refuse either to hear their beliefs or to be open to reexamining our own beliefs that we stray into a fundamentalist mindset.

Fortunately, evangelism is not one-sided. Evangelism is not about having the final answers and forcing people to accept them but about sharing authentically good news in a way that is meaningful to those who hear us. By being both reflective about our own beliefs and sensitive to the context in which we share the good news, we avoid becoming fundamentalist while staying true to our core beliefs.

By navigating evangelism so that we know what we believe, why we believe it and how we can share it in a sensitive way, we use the very practice of evangelism to dispel the negative views people hold about evangelism. Nothing displaces old notions better than new examples that prove those old notions wrong. We can provide people with evidence that evangelism is not propagating irrational beliefs or shutting down the quest for meaning. If we navigate well through these obstacles, people may be willing to hear about the good news that motivates our evangelistic activities.

PRACTICE

Evangelism was never meant to be a domesticated field of theological study. It is first and foremost an action. Most of the Greek words in the Bible from which we derive the English word "evangelism" are verbs. Biblically, evangelism is something we do, not a thing we consider. As important as the mental and spiritual work behind our practice of evangelism is, none of it matters if we do not act on these new insights. This is why navigating evangelism ultimately leads us to become practitioners of evangelism. We do not just generate useful practices; we become formed as authentic carriers of the good news we authentically hold and embody.

Given that evangelism calls for us to be formed by the good news, then the work we start in studying evangelism must continue beyond the classroom. Evangelism is not a subject to be studied so we can check it off the graduation grid, scratch it from the list of ordination requirements or meet some other external demand. It is a launching pad. We study evangelism with the expectation that we will continue charting our evangelistic course for the rest of our lives.

Our ongoing navigation of evangelism is necessary because our destination is an ever-moving one. We will never stop needing to reflect on what

LEARNING ACTIVITY

Moving between formal theological language and everyday language about what we believe can be difficult. It might be helpful to write a sermon or other short talk in which we describe our core beliefs to someone else who has not studied theology. This requires us to articulate our beliefs and our reasons for undertaking evangelism in simpler and more accessible language. Using this simpler language also helps us clarify what we believe.

we believe the good news to be, learning to relate to our context and translating the good news into creative practices. We will never master evangelism, but we can become expert pilots relating to the people around us with creativity, cultural awareness and an authentic way of articulating the good news.

This chapter has provided us with a basic sense of what to leave behind (our stereotypes) and what to watch out for (the influences of modernity, postmodernity and fundamentalist mindsets) in our voyage toward authentic evangelism. We've also been reminded that we will be navigating toward our destination well beyond our initial study. With this insight in place, we move forward onto our first major leg of the journey: articulating our starting point.

LEARNING ACTIVITY

While an evangelism course cannot measure how well we practice evangelism, it can help equip and inspire us to engage in evangelism once the course is over. First, course assignments can include practical work, such as case studies and congregational analyses. These can be especially helpful for those who are already in professional ministry settings or who are hoping to enter such settings by providing valuable classroom time to think about what sorts of evangelistic practices would be applicable to their situations. Second, courses can include field trips to a variety of ministry sites. These provide an opportunity to observe what evangelism looks like when practiced by Christians coming from different theological backgrounds doing ministry in different settings. These trips can offer practical insights on how to engage in evangelism as well as potential inspiration from the work others are doing. Third, the course can provide opportunities for students to meet denominational officials or other ministry leaders who can help them engage in evangelism in the future.

Chapter Two

Finding a Better Starting Point

Soon after I left for college, my home church was rocked by tragedy. One of the high school students in our youth group died in a car accident. Both she and her family had been active in the church for years. Several of the adults had watched her grow up and many of my peers in the church had been her long-time friends.

A year later, another high school girl died. This one was abducted and murdered. Her body was found in a wooded area a few miles from the church. She had begun attending youth group at our church a only few months earlier and was not as well known. Her family did not attend the church at all.

The church hosted the funerals for both girls, packing the sanctuary with large numbers of teenagers and community members. The pastors were sensitive and loving within these terrible circumstances, and the church members rallied around the heartbroken families.

A few days after the second service, I spoke with the youth pastor to ask how he was holding up since he had known both girls and had been the primary pastoral caregiver for the other students who were trying to make sense of what had happened. He confessed to being tired but he also said he was encouraged. Puzzled, I asked him why.

He related to me a conversation he'd had with the funeral director who had been involved with both services. This director had dealt with the deaths of children and youth before, and from those experiences he'd expected the services would be filled with grief. And that was true to a point. Certainly people were sad. What he did not expect was that the services were not defined by that grief. While acknowledging the pain caused by the loss of these girls, the services transcended that pain. Grounded in the firm conviction that Jesus Christ had conquered death through the resurrection, the pastors had witnessed in their words and the congregation had shown through its love that there was hope. He even thought a note of joy had crept into the services.

LEARNING ACTIVITY

Most people approach evangelism with the assumption that even if we do it well, it will fail. It is helpful to think about what will happen if our evangelism is successful, since this points us toward the ultimate good that should motivate us as our starting point. Ask yourself: If God fully transformed the person you were evangelizing, what would that mean for the person? What good thing would that person experience? What good things would God ultimately bring about in that person's life?

The funeral director told the youth pastor that he felt better about the world when he left the two services than when he had entered them. As he finished his story, the youth pastor smiled and said he was encouraged that the church had shared the hope and joy of Jesus Christ in the face of tragedy.

Knowing the people from my home church, I was not surprised at their ability to witness under such trying circumstances. They knew the core message that anchored their faith, that the resurrection of Jesus Christ is the ultimate good news of God. No matter what they had to address, the wellspring of this belief provided them with all they needed.

This core belief is what I refer to as the "starting point" in navigating evangelism.[1] The starting point is a distilled statement of what makes the good news good. When we can articulate this we are able to share that good news no matter how bad the world around us seems.

The starting point is also what motivates us to engage in evangelism. As we saw in the previous chapter, the barriers to sharing our faith with other

---

[1] I am indebted to Scott Jones for the terminology of "starting point." Scott J. Jones, *The Evangelistic Love of God and Neighbor: A Theology of Witness and Discipleship* (Nashville: Abingdon, 2003), 25.

people are high. If we are to navigate around them, we need a powerful motivation that inspires us on our journey toward an authentic understanding and practice of evangelism. Our starting point provides that. It gives us something so good to offer that we are willing to endure possible discomfort for the sake of sharing it with others. Put another way, when navigating evangelism, the starting point is our fixed North Star that we can look to for guidance and purpose regardless of what we face.

These two questions can help us find our starting point: (1) Why do we choose to remain Christian? (2) What is the good that we believe God wants to accomplish? We will take these two questions in turn.

WHY DO WE REMAIN CHRISTIAN?

In Western societies the number of people who advocate for others to follow Jesus Christ is dwindling. While many cultures make room for people who adhere to the Christian faith, and some cultures have vestiges of the Christian faith in them (e.g., the celebration of Christmas), we would be hard-pressed to find a culture that encourages people to live according to the teachings of Jesus. The invitation of Jesus to self-denial and suffering alone is enough to make most cultural value systems back away from following him too closely.

Added to this is the hypocrisy of the church. For a group of people who are supposed to be defined by the love of God and neighbor, the church is riddled with failures in living out these commitments. These come writ large (e.g., the Crusades, the Inquisition and leadership scandals) and small (e.g., congregational infighting, denominational bureaucratic wrangling and the inability of denominations to take a clear stance on hot-button social issues).

For these and other reasons, an increasing number of people have chosen not to affiliate with the Christian faith or any religion. These so-called nones (those who choose "none" on surveys asking them to identify their religion or faith tradition) are, since the early 2010s, the fastest-growing "religious" group in the United States. Their numbers are swelled by a hemorrhage of people who used to attend church and from a new generation of people who were never raised in a religious faith.

The result of all this is to make self-identification as Christian a less common phenomenon. This is why we need to begin the first leg of our journey toward an authentic understanding and practice of evangelism by asking why we remain Christian. Following Jesus Christ is not something we have to do. We could all walk away from Christ tomorrow and we would be met with the cheers of an increasingly secular culture for doing so.

I believe it is our experience of the overwhelming goodness of God that keeps us Christian. We have identified something that is so good it gives us meaning on a deep level. Without it the world would be a very different, much more painful place. It is for this reason we are willing to be identified with Jesus Christ publicly in spite of the shame we might face for doing so.[2]

If we have found something that good for us, we also have something good enough to share with others. Think of it this way: If we watch a movie we think is excellent, won't we tell our friends about it? Our friends would not think we were arrogant for forcing our personal taste in movies on them. They would accept that we saw something we liked and might even appreciate that we're sharing it with them. We are not forcing them to see it nor, if they do see it, are we condemning them if they disagree with our assessment of it. We are just sharing something that has been good for us.

Evangelism is similar. We are sharing something we have found to be good. Of course, evangelism goes deeper than encouraging someone to spend ten bucks and two hours watching a movie. The good news calls people to a new way of life. As such it is something we need to be careful in communicating (this goes back to the idea of evangelism being a bias). Even so, like the movie, it makes sense to share what we have found to be good with others.

It is not enough for evangelism to be motivated by our experiences of God's goodness in Jesus Christ, however. If this were our only motivation, then evangelism would fall into the trap of individualism laid by both modernity and postmodernity, with the individual evangelist's experience taking precedent over the content of the good news itself. As N. T. Wright warned, we would be offering only good advice instead of good news.

It is a fallacy to argue that the goodness of God is nothing more than what a person, or a group of people, thinks is good. God's goodness is not defined as "good" because a popular opinion poll has determined it to be so. It is good because the nature of God is good. God is the source of all that is good. This leads us to the second question.

---

[2]Mark R. Teasdale, "Enduring Shame as a Baseline for Conversion," *The Journal of Christian Ministry* 5 (2013), journalofchristianministry.org/article/view/11691.

What Is the Good God Wants to Accomplish?

Our belief in the ultimate is a powerful motivator. What we think will happen in the end defines what we do now. We work hard to get good grades because we know ultimately we will receive a diploma for it. We seek higher education or training because we believe ultimately it will increase our vocational opportunities and earning potential. We discipline our children because we believe that ultimately it will teach them to make better choices. The end goals drive our decisions about what we do now. This is no different when we are thinking about God.

A common belief Christians hold across the theological spectrum is that God has a plan. For some of us this plan has a clearly defined end. For others the plan is for God to walk alongside of creation, prompting its inhabitants to live in a way that leads to humanity and creation flourishing. Regardless of what this plan looks like for us individually, all Christians hold that God is engaged intentionally with creation, and this engagement is to bring about good. What we believe this good looks like directly influences how and why we evangelize.

Defining what we think is the ultimate work of God differs from identifying the good that keeps us Christian. The latter explains how we personally receive the good news. The former makes a claim about the purpose and order of the universe itself. We are making a normative claim about the way God wants things to be.

This is the point that raises many people's worst fears about evangelism. Evangelism, they think, demands a competition between the evangelist and the evangelized in which only one will have their initial beliefs remain. The evangelist wants to expunge the evangelized's existing beliefs about the purpose and meaning of the world, replacing those beliefs with his or her own.

We should not deny that evangelists seek to augment or replace people's existing beliefs. Evangelism entails sharing the good news of God with the hope that people will hear it and receive it. If the person believes something that is harmful toward others or inaccurate about God, then we want the person to accept the good news in place of those beliefs. By the same token, an evangelist should never condemn people. As evangelists we invite others to consider and be challenged by the good news of God in Jesus Christ. We do not issue a blanket condemnation of those who disagree with that good news.

The difficulty many of us have in dealing with this nuance is that evangelism has traditionally been understood as dealing in propositions. The evangelist makes propositional truth claims about who God is and how people must respond to God. The evangelized must either accept or reject these truth claims, with no means of engaging in thoughtful dialogue with the evangelist. We can overcome this by understanding that evangelism trades in stories more than in propositions. This is because stories have more capacity to convey nuanced and meaningful goodness to people than propositions do.[3]

Philosopher Alasdair MacIntyre contended that one of the best ways to understand human lives is to view them through the lens of narrative.[4] While his argument is focused on how groups of people develop common narratives, his point holds true for individuals. Most of us make sense of our lives by weaving them into a story. That story is our life story, the sum total of all that has happened to us and is happening. We are the main character, and a host of secondary, tertiary and other characters come in and out of the story. We know something of our beginning and how we got to where we are. We also have some sense of where we are going and what we would like the ending to be. How good, bad or successful we think we are in life is defined relative to what we think our life's story should be.

To make these value judgments, we need a story that is bigger than our personal life story. We need something that provides us with a larger perspective that we can use to fold around our personal narrative. This larger story is called a metanarrative. Just as everyone has their own life story, so everyone has a metanarrative.

A metanarrative is an overarching story that we tell about the universe and how it operates. If our personal narrative explains the who, what, when and how of our lives, the metanarrative explains the why.[5] It gives us a sense of order, providing the framework for finding meaning in life and the reasons for why our lives and the world around us have unfolded as they

---

[3]Richard B. Hays, *The Moral Vision of the New Testament: Community, Cross, New Creation* (New York: HarperOne, 1996), 73.

[4]Alasdair MacIntyre, "The Virtues, the Unity of a Human Life, and the Concept of a Tradition," in *After Virtue: A Study in Moral Theory* (Notre Dame, IN: University of Notre Dame Press, 1984), 204-25.

[5]People's narratives and metanarratives are also influenced by cultural and social factors. We will take up this issue in the chapter on context.

have. It gives us a way to deal with things outside our control. It also provides a basis for claiming things to be right, wrong, good or bad.

A metanarrative can stretch wide enough to encompass the destiny of the universe, giving us a picture of the ultimate. From this idea of how everything will turn out in the end, we gain a sense of purpose, and that purpose filters down into our daily lives. The grand conclusion of the metanarrative becomes the subtext that forms us and informs all we do. For example, if we believe that ultimately existence will culminate in the rise of the eternal chicken empire that will render judgment on all humans, it will have an impact on which restaurants we eat in now. We will act in accordance with what we think we will have to give an account for ultimately.

A caveat: The concept of metanarratives fell out of fashion with the rise of postmodernity. In modernity, the prevailing metanarratives reduced humans to little more than mechanisms or functions of nature. This came as a result of Newtonian physics and Enlightenment philosophy, which concluded that everything could be defined by measurable phenomena. It left no room for mystery or the supernatural. As such, personal narratives, as interesting as they might be, were little more than color commentary in a deterministic metanarrative that saw the world and its inhabitants as cogs in a great machine. Postmodernity rightly rejected this.

However, this rejection of modernity's mechanistic metanarrative did not end people's need to make sense of why the universe operates the way it does or why things happen in their lives the way they do. Instead of ending the metanarrative altogether, postmodernity individualized it. Rather than being expected to conform to a single metanarrative, each person now has his or her own personal metanarrative. These personal metanarratives can be as reductionistic as those on offer during modernity, or they can espouse the mystical, mysterious and supernatural. Regardless of the content, metanarratives are still a going concern.

One way to understand evangelism is as a call for people to shift their metanarratives. It is an invitation for them to make sense of their personal lives based on a new way of understanding how the universe operates. Specifically, it invites someone to consider what it means to acknowledge the God of Jesus Christ as the central actor in the universe and reorienting their life around God.

In inviting people to consider this new metanarrative, we in no way dismiss a person's individual narrative. Evangelism should acknowledge and appreciate each person's life story. What possible reason could we have for disputing people's descriptions of what happened to them over the course of their lives? We want to help them navigate toward a new meaning and

LEARNING ACTIVITY

The line exercise is a simple way to help us see how our personal narratives and our metanarratives connect.

1. Draw a line that represents your life. It should include peaks, valleys and plateaus to represent the high, low and mundane periods of your life.

2. Once you have finished your line, label the parts of it that are most important to you.

3. After you have added these first labels, write what you believe God was doing during those same moments. This should be based on your current understanding of what God was doing in your life, not on what you thought God was doing at the time those periods of your life occurred.

Once you have finished, you have an integrated depiction of your personal narrative and your metanarrative. You have explained your life and have also shown how you used your metanarrative about God to make sense of what happened in your life. A secondary result of this activity is that you have shown that you are equipped to serve as an evangelist. All people have peaks, valleys and plateaus. An evangelist's job is not to refute this or try to explain away those instances but to share how the metanarrative of Jesus Christ can make sense of peaks, valleys and plateaus.

This is not something to force on others but an invitation to consider what it would look like for someone to reconsider their own life through the lens of a Christian metanarrative. This understanding of evangelism helps overcome the fear many people have of not being prepared or educated enough to evangelize. We do not need the answers. We just need to articulate how the good news of God through Jesus Christ has made sense of our personal stories.

purpose through the good news of God, just as we navigated to that place. We want them to recognize that, just as Jesus promised in the Great Commission, God has always been active in their lives. We are not bringing God to them but, as evangelist Leonard Sweet puts it, are "nudging" them to see the signs of how God's story has been weaving through their stories all along.[6]

Evangelism also does not seek to condemn people for the metanarratives they already accept. Nowhere are we charged to tell people they are wrong, stupid or foolish in their thinking. Although evangelism does resist and condemn metanarratives that are harmful to people (e.g., a metanarrative that assumes certain groups are superior to others, such as in racism or sexism), it would never claim that the person who held that metanarrative was of less worth than other people or automatically condemned by God. Again, it bears repeating that evangelism rejects no person and condemns only beliefs that prevent people from accessing the redemptive goodness of God. This is why God's news is good news for all people, even for those who disagree with it.

What is the ultimate good we believe God wants to bring about, and how does that belief in the ultimate shape our metanarrative? Our answer to this question is a critical part of navigating our way through evangelism by helping us determine our starting point.

THINKING BIG

As we answer our questions about the goodness of God that inspires us to remain Christians and motivates us to share our faith, we need to think big. Metanarratives that include visions of the ultimate work of God should not be small. A small metanarrative equates to a small starting point, and a small starting point equates to belief in a small God. If we are going to navigate to an authentic understanding and practice of evangelism that will transform others' lives, we need to steer toward big answers to the two questions we have just discussed.

Small starting points usually amount to little more than tenets for how to live. Instead of inviting people to interpret their personal life stories in a new way, we give them a set of beliefs or activities that we claim are necessary to

---

[6]Leonard Sweet, *Nudge: Awakening Each Other to the God Who's Already There* (Colorado Springs: David C. Cook, 2010), 28-29.

become Christians. We offer propositions to accept instead of narratives to embody. The result of these starting points is that our evangelism becomes moralistic rather than inviting.

Much evangelism today does not have a big enough starting point. This is because many evangelism texts and programs are focused on how we practice evangelism without asking why we do it. Denominational and congregational evangelistic programs are frequently guilty of this, telling members they should be evangelists without helping them discern any reason for their evangelism other than the need to recruit more members.[7]

It is the very people we hope to invite into God's goodness who suffer the most when our starting points are too small. Those who accept our message end up engaging in a partial practice of the Christian faith or having a partial commitment to the Christian faith. Our small starting points hamstring the next generation of Christians.

Small starting points have already damaged the church. A chief example is the steady decline of people in the United States who identify with a specific Christian tradition. According to the Pew Research Center, each generation of Americans is less connected to the Christian faith than the previous: 85 percent of those born between 1928 and 1945 claim to be Christian; 78 percent of those born between 1946 and 1964 claim the same, along with 70 percent of those born between 1965 and 1980, 57 percent of those born between 1981 and 1989, and 56 percent of those born between 1990 and 1998.[8]

The same study showed that even those who do claim the Christian faith are not secure in that identity. Religious switching, which occurs when a person leaves one category of religious identity for another, is working against most churches, with people leaving in larger numbers than they are joining. The only exception to this is what Pew identifies as the "evangelical" church.[9]

But even within the evangelical tradition there are troubles. A different study of the young adult population in the United States showed that while

---

[7] An excellent analysis of this for the United Methodist Church can be found in Heather Heinzman Lear, "Reclaiming Evangelism: Evaluating the Effect of Evangelism Understanding and Practice on Discipleship in Selected United Methodist Congregations" (DMin diss., Garrett-Evangelical Theological Seminary, 2015).

[8] Pew Research Center, *America's Changing Religious Landscape* (Washington, DC: Pew Research Center, 2015), 11.

[9] Ibid., 35.

there is a group within this demographic who declared themselves to be very conservative in their beliefs, the people in this group acknowledged that they had difficulty ordering their lives around those beliefs.[10]

What is causing this? While recognizing that there are numerous factors behind these findings, from the vantage point of evangelism I would argue that the primary problem has been too small of a starting point. Without a powerful metanarrative to guide people, they have been left with vague notions of God that are not sufficient to make sense of or give purpose to their lives.

Throughout the twentieth century, the churches in the United States have modified the good news they have preached to accommodate cultural values. In doing this the church has put itself in a reactive posture to the culture instead of presenting itself with an identity strong enough to reform the culture. As a result the church has conducted its evangelism from a shrinking starting point. That in turn has presented a less compelling metanarrative to each generation of Americans, making it easier for them to turn away from the church or at least harder for them to accept the discipline required by the Christian faith.

Small starting points have an even more sinister impact than diminishing the attraction of the Christian faith. They also promote counterfeit versions of the faith. Kenda Creasy Dean, drawing on the National Study of Youth and Religion, argues this point in her book *Almost Christian*. She asks pointedly:

> What if the church models a way of life that asks, not passionate surrender but ho-hum assent? What if we are preaching moral affirmation, a feel-better faith, and a hands-off God instead of the decisively involved, impossibly loving, radically sending God of Abraham and Mary, who desired us enough to enter creation in Jesus Christ and whose Spirit is active in the church and in the world today?[11]

According to Dean, if this is all the church has to offer, it stops sowing the seeds of the Christian faith and plants moralistic therapeutic deism (MTD) instead. The term MTD was coined by youth researchers Christian Smith and

---

[10]Beth Seversen and Rick Richardson, "Emerging Adults and the Future of Evangelism," *Witness: Journal of the Academy for Evangelism in Theological Education* 28 (2014): 47-48.

[11]Kenda Creasy Dean, *Almost Christian: What the Faith of Our Teenagers is Telling the American Church* (New York: Oxford University Press, 2010), 12.

Melinda Denton to describe what masquerades as the Christian faith in many American churches in the early twenty-first century. It is a belief system that calls us to be nice, hopes that God will help when we are in need but otherwise prefers God to stay out of the way, and believes that the good God wants to accomplish is to make us feel good about ourselves both now and in heaven.[12] It requires no sacrifices and no discipleship.

So how do we avoid having a starting point that is too small? We must ground our starting point in the character and activity of God. Our evangelism should always begin with the goodness that flows from God, never with human activity.

The problem is that we often want to start the process of evangelism by looking at what we can accomplish and measure as humans. There is a veritable cottage industry promoted by seminaries, research institutes and denominational studies that looks for best practices to maximize people's positive response to evangelism. There is nothing inherently wrong with these studies. However, when we turn these practices into our starting point, we get into trouble.

Practices are just that—they are practices. They are means of living into a vision. They are not supposed to be the vision itself. When we confuse the practices and the vision, we confuse the means with the end. This is problematic for evangelism. Evangelism does not exist to further its own practice or even to further the practices of the church. Evangelism exists to invite people into the good news of God. Therefore evangelism needs to be founded on the good news of who God is and how God operates in our world, not on how humans can do things to reach out to God.

To use our navigation metaphor, we chart our course to faithful practices only after we have articulated the goodness those practices need to convey. To begin our voyage with the practices would be to navigate backwards, trying to force our views of God to fit with the activities we've chosen.

In teaching my class on evangelism, I often pose a variety of possible starting points. These include "service evangelism" (which focuses on calling people to the good news through doing loving acts for them), "anthro-evangelism" (a catchall term I use to describe evangelism focused on meeting

---

[12]Ibid., 14.

people's felt needs, such as entertainment evangelism), and apologetics (which tries to convince others of propositional truth claims about God and Jesus Christ). I explain that none of these are wrong as practices. Christians should engage in loving acts toward others, meet the needs of others and be able to articulate why they believe what they believe. The problem arises when Christians make these practices their starting points.

When we use human activity as our starting point, it diminishes the metanarrative of the people we evangelize if they accept our message. The servant evangelist and the anthro-evangelist end up with people who have come to know Jesus as a personal savior but who are ill-equipped to deal with the tragedies of life. At best their reduced Christian metanarrative falls apart in the face of trials and tribulations. At worst their faith turns venomous by suggesting that if the person had just believed more they would have been safe from problems. The apologist might convince someone to accept certain propositions but not provide the person with ways to deal with noncognitive issues that arise in daily life. In each case the starting point proves too small to develop a full-fledged metanarrative of the Christian faith that can guide one's personal narrative.

Contrast these starting points to two others. One is the kingdom of God and the other is the nature of God.[13] The former points to one way of describing God's ultimate purpose, that of setting all things right in heaven and on earth. The latter points to the person of God, emphasizing God's character. Unlike the previous three, these starting points do not have clear practices connected to them. They allow for a wide array of creative evangelistic practices to demonstrate the goodness of God. They are also immersive. People who are presented with a metanarrative grounded in the kingdom of God or the nature of God find ample room to reinterpret their personal life stories within its vastness. They are not just adhering to a few rules; they are conforming their lives to a grand, all-encompassing vision of God's goodness.

William Abraham in *The Logic of Evangelism* offers a good example of evangelism based on God's activity. Using the kingdom of God as his starting point, Abraham develops a comprehensive catechetical process for initiating a person into the kingdom. He argues that for evangelism to be effective, it

---

[13]Jones, *Evangelistic Love*, 27, 33.

has to connect people's lives to six aspects of the kingdom.[14] These aspects
are: (1) the experiential, (2) the communal, (3) the cognitive, (4) the moral,
(5) the vocational and (6) spiritual disciplines. Abraham goes so far as to argue
that people evangelized with only some of these aspects become "malformed"
Christians.[15] Those initiated into the kingdom in all six ways have everything
they need for their lives to be reinterpreted by the Christian faith.

Whether or not we agree with Abraham's entire thesis, we can acknowledge that he demonstrates the importance of a grand starting point
by showing how it opens the door for a broad range of evangelistic activities
that transform the whole person. A person evangelized in this way will have
a sense of who God is and what God is doing in every aspect of life.

Starting points based on human activity reduce the vision of God for those
being evangelized. This results in only partial commitment to and practice of
the Christian faith. Starting points based in God's nature and activity offer God
in all God's grandeur and invite the evangelized to receive a metanarrative
large enough to transform every aspect of one's personal narrative.

The first Christians had a large starting point in mind when they launched
their evangelistic efforts. It was the unalloyed joyful good news that God had
raised Jesus Christ from the dead and offered this same resurrection to all
who followed Jesus. This good news spurred them to claim their own faith
and offer that faith to others. This idea of death being upended and a new
life beginning in Christ was a huge starting point then. It remains so today.

Our starting point is our authentic belief about what is so good about
God that we continue to identify as followers of Jesus Christ. It is also something so great and wonderful that it offers us a powerful vision of God's
purposes for the universe.

There is something powerful about being able to articulate this core belief.
It not only motivates us to share the good we have with others but it can
soothe our own souls to be able to claim it. As Howard Thurman wrote,

> How good it is to center down! To sit quietly and see one's self pass by! The
> streets of our minds seethe with endless traffic; our spirits resound with
> clashings, with noisy silences, while something deep within hungers and
> thirsts for the still moment and the resting lull. With full intensity we seek, ere

---

[14]Abraham, *Logic of Evangelism*, 101-103.
[15]Ibid., 140.

the quiet passes, a fresh sense of order in our living; A direction, a strong sure purpose that will structure our confusion and bring meaning in our chaos. We look at ourselves in this waiting moment—the kinds of people we are. The questions persist: what are we doing with our lives?—what are the motives that order our days? What is the end of our doings? Where are we trying to go? Where do we put the emphasis and where are our values focused? For what end do we make sacrifices? Where is my treasure and what do I love most in life? What do I hate most in life and to what am I true? Over and over the questions beat in upon the waiting moment. As we listen, floating up through all the jangling echoes of our turbulence, there is a sound of another kind—A deeper not which only the stillness of the heart makes clear. It moves directly to the core of our being. Our questions are answered, with the peace of the Eternal in our step. How good it is to center down![16]

While having articulated our starting point is an excellent step forward, there is more work for us to do. Terms we might use in our starting points like "the kingdom of God" and "the nature of God" can easily become so big that their meanings get lost. To avoid this, evangelists must be careful to define these terms in reference to the good news they desire to share. Articulating these definitions is the work of theology, to which we now turn.

---

[16]Howard Thurman, *Meditations of the Heart* (Boston: Beacon Press, 1999), 28.

Chapter Three

Looking Inward
to Look Outward

*I*t was a beautiful Saturday morning when I left with a group of friends to attend a large Christian rally being held in a professional football stadium. The event boasted several nationally known singers and speakers, and we arrived early to get seats on the field near the stage. We were successful, and we settled in for a good day.

The rally started with a concert followed by several stirring sermons. We appreciated and agreed with what we were hearing. The way the speakers explained the Bible resonated with what we already believed about God, convicted us of our shortcomings and encouraged us to grow in our faith.

As the day continued, we began to notice a slight shift in the air. Glancing through the open roof of the stadium, we could see clouds gather. Unexpectedly, the sky erupted. A downpour soaked us, along with all the others who had been fortunate enough to find seats on the field. Without anywhere to go, we used anything we could find to deflect the rain. We also huddled closer together as we watched the large thermometer in the stadium sink nearly twenty degrees in about thirty minutes. Several of us helped one of our number, an elderly gentleman with a variety of health problems, off the field and into a dry area on the side of the stadium.

The rally had not stopped during all of this. The band had come back on stage in an effort to lift attendees' flagging morale. The worship leader for the event took the mic and began to yell cheerily, "We should bless God. It's just liquid sunshine!" My friends and I, who felt neither warmed nor brightened by this alternative form of sunshine, were not so certain. Perhaps it was easier to see the positives of this squall from under a roof with sweatshirts and towels readily available than it was in the open with no resources to forestall the effects of the weather.

This incident marked the first time I understood the importance of theological reflection. Growing up I had always believed it was enough to know the core tenets of my faith. I never reflected on how those beliefs came to be and why I should believe them. But faced with these contrasting interpretations of the weather from those getting rained on and those who remained dry, I became suspicious that Christian faithfulness required more than just believing the right things.

The second leg of our journey in navigating evangelism involves reflecting theologically on our starting point. In doing this we define and possibly modify our beliefs in conversation with the Christian Tradition and a variety of theological traditions. In the process we become more capable of articulating what we believe to be the good news in a way that is authentic to our view of God's goodness.

CHRISTIAN TRADITION AND THEOLOGICAL TRADITIONS

Navigating through theological reflection is necessarily contextual. We can never break free from the time and place in which we live, so our theology cannot either. This is excellent from the standpoint of evangelism! The revelation of God can be spoken anew to each culture in each historical era without losing its potency. The good news of God will always be good news regardless of where or when we are called on to share it.

The contextual nature of theology makes it especially important that we consult church tradition. Without tradition, contextualization can cause us to slip into the arrogance of thinking we know enough about God without anyone else's insight and so confusing the revelation of God with political, economic or other agendas.[1] By holding ourselves accountable to the traditions of the church we avoid this mistake.

Even the notion of tradition is tricky, though. Timothy Ware, a Greek Orthodox bishop, explains that we must differentiate between big-t "Tradition" and small-t "traditions." The big-t Tradition is the rich inheritance all Christians receive in the form of the Bible, the ecumenical councils, the

---

[1]See G. K. Chesterton's *Orthodoxy* for a smashing response to those who dismiss tradition because it is based on the beliefs held by people from long ago who are now dead.

creeds and even the basic structure of the church. Small-t traditions are other opinions we inherit.[2] Both Tradition and traditions provide a pattern for how we should live and so can become tangled. Both also shape our theology. For this reason, we need to be clear about which one we are deploying in our theological reflection.

Small-t traditions often create specialized categories within the big-t Tradition. These traditions can be ethnic (the Serbian Orthodox Church, the Russian Orthodox Church), racial (the black church), political (a "conservative" church or a "liberal" church) or something else. Appending these traditions to our understanding of the Tradition will bring us to differing views of the Christian faith. It is from these views that the various theological traditions (evangelicalism, liberation theology) spring.

Some theological traditions seek to deconstruct other traditions they consider harmful or coercive (for example, black theologians have argued that the white-dominated theology in the West often makes assumptions about God and humanity that privileges white people). Other theological traditions address aspects of the Christian faith that are seen as lacking in more prominent traditions (e.g., liberation theology sought to sensitize people to God's call for justice at a time when Western theology focused on waiting for God to set all things right in the end).

Navigating evangelism means reflecting on our beliefs through as many of these traditions as we can, learning how to articulate our beliefs with the guidance the traditions provide. It means discovering which traditions are most comfortable to us as well as being open to the critiques of traditions that make us uncomfortable.

At the same time that theological reflection helps us articulate our faith, it also helps us overcome the tendency to vilify traditions we do not agree with. If we approach all traditions with the assumption that they are grounded in the good news, we can find ways to be more generous in how we relate to Christians across the theological spectrum. This is a point we will consider in detail at the end of this chapter.

Recognizing that the Christian Tradition—as expressed in a variety of theological traditions—maps out how we can organize our thoughts about

---

[2]Timothy Ware, *The Orthodox Church* (New York: Penguin, 1993), 196.

the good news, we are better prepared to navigate through theological reflection toward an authentic understanding and practice of evangelism. Still, before we explicitly consult different theological traditions to reflect on the good news, we would be wise to get a sense of what our gut-level beliefs are. We may decide not to keep these beliefs, but beginning with them gives us clarity and authenticity about the message we want to share with others.

There are two broad areas we need to reflect on to clarify what we already believe. First we need to consider the content of what we believe. Second we have to explain why we believe these things. We will address each of these in turn.

WHAT: THREE CORE QUESTIONS

Theological reflection seeks to answer three basic questions about the content of our Christian beliefs:

1. Who is God?

2. What does God do?

3. How do we respond to God based on who God is and what God does?

When we reflect on these questions it is critical that we stay focused on our starting point. The starting point is like our face, something that is authentically our own. Theological reflection is like the process of examining our face as it appears to us in a mirror. We look at our beliefs about God, God's actions and human response as they arise from our starting point.

Theological traditions, when we begin to use them, are like different perspectives we can take when looking in the mirror. Just as looking at our faces from different angles in a mirror provides us different information on what we need to do to make ourselves more presentable (e.g., brush our hair, clean our teeth), so considering our beliefs through different theological traditions gives us ways of seeing potential flaws, gaps or blind spots in our beliefs we might not have seen in our initial reflection. The more theological traditions we use to reflect on our starting point, the more insight we will gain about it.

During our reflection we should be consistent in our vocabulary. If, for example, we state that we are motivated to evangelize by our belief in the kingdom of God, then we should always use the term "kingdom of God" as we pose the questions. Who is the kind of God that would establish a kingdom? How will God establish this kingdom? What does it mean that God desires to establish this kingdom? How is the establishment of the kingdom good for people? How would people participate in this kingdom? This sort of questioning may seem tedious, but it keeps our reflection focused on our starting point. Staying consistent in our vocabulary will help us stay on course as we navigate toward authentic evangelism.

Maintaining a consistent vocabulary is also important because theology is like a spiderweb. Each belief is connected to the others. No belief can be modified without the others being changed. Using our example of the kingdom of God, our answer to who God is should correspond to our answer for what it means for God to establish a kingdom. The nature of God (under the "Who is God?" question) should be consistent with the actions of God (under the "What does God do?" question). If there is disjunction among the answers, we should retrace our thinking to see where the points of disagreement are and consider why they are there. This helps keep our theological reflection coherent.

To begin the process of theological reflection, let's look at each question and how the church has classically answered it. Different theological traditions will provide different answers, but this initial foray will furnish us with some ideas on how we might answer these questions for ourselves.

1. Who is God? The first question deals with the doctrine of God. It asks about the nature of God both in terms of God's existence and character. For the earliest theologians, answering this question meant wrestling with the doctrine of the Trinity. They concluded that God is three-in-one; the Father, Son and Holy Spirit are three distinct persons who are one in essence and equally God.

In working out the three-in-oneness of God, the question arises of what common character traits exist among all the persons of the Trinity. Are all three equally powerful? Are all three equally wise? Are all three equally compassionate or judgmental? Other questions also present themselves: To what extent does each person participate in the activities of God? Does each have a unique realm of activity or do all three inseparably participate in all activities?

An important lesson we can learn from how the church has addressed this question is that each answer opens new areas of inquiry that cross doctrinal categories. In speaking to the doctrine of God, for example, the church also deals with Christology and pneumatology. The nature of the Trinity cannot be separated from Jesus Christ and the Holy Spirit. This is the spiderweb nature of theology, with each belief prompting us to clarify other beliefs.

When navigating evangelism, we need to reflect on how the nature of God relates to the good news we claim in our starting point. Since our starting point is focused on the good news of God, we might reasonably begin our reflection by positing that God is good. If we believe that God has an ultimate way of establishing that good, then we could also posit that God is powerful. We could use these initial answers as jumping-off points to explore how the goodness and power of God work through God's trinitarian existence. This is just one possible way forward.

As we determine what God's nature is like, we are prodded to ask the next question: What does a God with this kind of nature do?

2. *What does God do?* When they were younger, my children would often ask me if a new character introduced in a movie we were watching was a good guy or a bad guy. Their reason for doing this was to have a framework for interpreting the actions of that character throughout the film. Bad guys inevitably did bad things while good guys did good things.

While simplistic, this logic is not too far off the mark in theological reflection. If we understand God's character to be good, loving and compassionate then we have reason to believe that God's actions will likewise be good, loving and compassionate. For a simple example, let us return to the possible starting point of the kingdom of God.

If we believe God is good, loving and compassionate, then we have a sense for what the process of establishing the kingdom will be like. It will be a process that is caring, quite different from the violence that the world usually witnesses during the replacing of one kingdom with another. Likewise, the kingdom itself will be a place of love and compassion, not one where people submit out of fear that they will be condemned by an insecure God who rules by force. This is especially true if we wed the belief that God is all-powerful to the belief that God is good and loving. Such a God has no fear of being overthrown and can move ahead unobstructed with establishing a kingdom organized around love rather than force. In making these observations we are dealing with eschatology, the study of God's purposes.

This broad area of inquiry also leads us to ask questions about how God relates to creation. Given the nature of God we have posited, what can we say about the nature of creation? What purpose did God have in creating, and what purpose does God desire for the creation? More specifically, what does God intend for humanity, which is unique within creation?

In introducing humanity, we introduce a new set of characters into the discussion. Like God, these characters have the ability to think and act as well as a nature all their own. So the question of how God relates to humanity is based not only on what God is like but on what humanity is like. Traditionally, Christians have understood humans to be created by God in the image of God (the *imago Dei*). What does it mean for humans to be created in God's image? Are we meant to be social, just as God lives in community by being three in one? Are we powerful, if not all-powerful like God? Are we fundamentally good, compassionate and loving just as God is?

Whatever we think God created humanity to be, the Christian faith proclaims that God desires to relate to humans. This leads us to soteriology, which speaks to how God opens the door for humans to enter into the fullness of God's goodness. It also points to both Christology and pneumatology as we look at how Jesus Christ and the Holy Spirit are part of God's salvific plan for us.

This is a simplified way of moving through these questions, but it again shows how the spiderweb of theology works. As we answer one question, seeking to articulate what we believe about who God is, we raise new questions about what God has done and inform our answers to those new questions with the answers we already have.

3. How do we respond to God based on who God is and what God does? While God desires for humans to share in God's goodness, humans have the ability to choose whether they will accept or reject God's offer. Theological reflection must address this. What options do humans have in dealing with God and what are the results of pursuing those options?

One option is to resist, reject or ignore the good God offers humanity. This option is understood as evil and is examined in hamartiology, or the study of sin. Another option is to seek God's goodness. This brings us to another aspect of soteriology, which not only details how God offers salvation to humanity but how humans can participate in that salvation.

A great many questions arise from looking at both hamartiology and soteriology. This is also the point at which theological traditions tend to differ. Virtually all theological traditions accept the answers to who God is and what God has done as a common inheritance from the big-t Christian Tradition. The question of how we are to respond to God has led to disagreement because our answers to these questions directly inform how we lead our lives and organize ourselves as churches.

Do we have freedom to choose sin or salvation or are we born with a predilection for one over the other? This gets into the idea of original sin. Does God need to intervene to enable us to turn away from sin and choose the good? Most theological traditions believe God must empower us to choose the good. The term used to describe that empowerment is "grace."

How do we respond to grace? Do we accept it or must we do something to earn it? Is it something we receive at a single point in time guaranteeing we will forever participate in God's goodness or is it something we have to continue to receive over time?

The classical Christian teaching is that the appropriate response to grace is for us to have faith in God. What does a response of faith look like? Is this response something we offer individually? Is there a corporate element to it? Does corporate faith have something to do with the church? If so, this pushes us to ecclesiology, which is the study of the church. What does a faithful church look like? Are there specific practices or beliefs that it must incorporate? What about some of the most long-standing practices like preaching and the sacraments? Are these activities means by which God delivers grace to people or are they responses to the grace God has already given—or are they both? What about issues of ordination and hierarchy and administration?

Does responding to God also entail treating people in a certain way? Does God's trinitarian existence and care of creation call us to live in community with other Christians and reach out in love beyond the Christian community? To rephrase this, if God has a mission of demonstrating goodness to all people, and if we are invited to participate in that goodness through grace, are we also incorporated into the mission of being gracious to other people as God has been gracious to us? What would participating in this mission look like? Does it entail meeting physical and emotional needs, telling people about God and the goodness God wants to share, helping overcome instances of evil and sin that we see harming people, or something else?

As we answer these questions, it becomes clear that theology is far from an esoteric pursuit. Our beliefs inexorably move toward practical application. This leads us back to the process of navigating evangelism, which ends in an authentic practice of evangelism. Before we do that, though, we have more theological reflection to do. Having answered the questions, we need to reflect on how we arrived at our answers. Specifically, we need to consider what sources we have privileged in our answers.

WHY: REVELATION AND INTERPRETATION

Theological reflection calls on us to reflect both on what we believe and why we believe it. Answering the three questions deals with the what. Discerning what led us to those beliefs deals with the why. To answer this question we need to identify: (1) the sources we drew our beliefs from and (2) how we interpreted those sources.

The answers to these questions are not easily uncovered. Yet leaving them unexplored causes us to have a hole in our evangelism. If we cannot explain why we believe what we do, it can cause difficulties when we share the goodness of God with others both outside and inside the church.

Divine revelation. In many theological treatises, both current and past, the author begins with the issue of how humans can know anything about God. If we believe God is beyond human comprehension, how can humans make legitimate claims to know anything about God, much less provide clear answers to the questions of who God is, what God does and how we respond?

The only way we can claim knowledge about God is to rely on an authority that provides accurate information about God. And since the most reliable authority that can speak about God is one that comes directly from God, we must have access to communication by God about God. This kind of communication in which God self-discloses information about God's nature, purposes and will is called "divine revelation."

Evangelism insists that we explain what sources we hold to be divine revelation for two reasons. First, since evangelism is a bias for the good news of God, we need to define that bias based on God's own description of the good news. Second, if a person accepts the good news we share, that person will need guidance on how to live according to the good news. Divine revelation is the primary resource we can offer for this.

Christians throughout history have pointed to the Bible as divine revelation. However, it is not enough for us to claim the Bible as our sole authority and leave it at that. Even if the Bible is our primary source of divine revelation, most Christians believe that God self-discloses in other ways as well. We need to be clear about which of these sources we use.

A helpful way to discern what other sources we classify as divine revelation is to differentiate between two approaches to theology. Kataphatic theology uses words to describe God, affirming what God has revealed. This is the approach of theological education, with its heavy emphasis on reading, writing, speaking and other means of communication among people about God. It is the type of theology most comfortable to Western Christians, especially to Protestants with their mantra of *sola Scriptura* and their focus on the sermon in worship.

The second approach is apophatic theology. It emphasizes knowing God through silence and contemplation, denying that human thought is adequate to describe the true nature of God. This is more commonly seen in the Eastern Church and among monastics who value spiritual practices such as prayer and meditation. Rather than looking to the words of others to help describe God, this approach listens for how God reveals the divine life directly to our interior lives.

Both approaches to theology are necessary. The kataphatic pushes us to articulate our beliefs, utilizing human reason and bending language to the cause of knowing God better. The apophatic brings us before the mysterious vastness of God, humbling us in our intellectual pursuits and reminding us that we cannot hope to know God unless we first learn to be quiet in God's presence.

Both approaches draw from the Bible as divine revelation, the kataphatic in order to study it and the apophatic to meditate on it. From there they diverge in what they recommend to us as divine revelation. Those who favor kataphatic theology are drawn to sources that offer well-reasoned ideas and words about God. This is not because kataphatic theology holds human reason or writing about God to be revelatory in its own right but because it believes God can use humans to communicate in an authoritative way. It is God's action through people that can make their work revelatory.

Apophatic theology is open to God communicating to humans in more direct ways. These include movements of the Holy Spirit through personal experiences, dreams, visions and other ways in which God is present to a person. These situations are often termed "mystical" and are possible for anyone to experience. As people enter into the presence of God and are attentive to God's voice, they can receive divine revelation.

Just as kataphatic theology does not baptize human reason, apophatic theology does not suggest that every experience is revelatory. To decide that a human experience is divine revelation without showing how God initiated that experience is to misapply apophatic theology. And this runs afoul of Jesus' stark warning that what comes out of a person is unclean (Mk 7:20-23).

In our theological reflection we need to ask ourselves if we favor one of these approaches. The two are not mutually exclusive, though most people are attracted to one over the other. Based on this, what sources do we grant the status of divine revelation? Are there writings by specific theologians or mystical experiences we have had that we hold as indispensable in answering the three questions of who God is, what God has done and how we respond?

Our authenticity will be that much greater if we can explain what we identify as divine revelation. Those we share the good news with will not just hear us espousing a new metanarrative for their lives; they will hear how we came to claim this metanarrative for ourselves. We will be vulnerable in sharing how we believe we heard from God, and that will be more attractive to our listeners.

Our theological reflection does not end with recognizing the sources we claim as divine revelation, though. We also need to be clear about how we interpret those sources.

An interpretive matrix. I remember my third grade Sunday school teacher emphasizing the importance of having a daily "quiet time" with God. This quiet time could include prayer, Bible reading, Bible memorization and even praising God with songs. The important thing was to make room to speak and listen to God each day.

Divine revelation is closely connected to having a quiet time. A quiet time is a means of mediating our communion with God, listening to God through the sources of revelation God has provided and using those same sources as a pattern for how to pray. The one thing it would seem we do not have to worry about during a quiet time is a filter between God and us. After all, if we sit down and read the Bible for ourselves, are we not directly grasping the meaning of what God is saying to us without any interference?

When God speaks to us, God does not bypass our reason or our feelings. God expects us to engage with God's whole message with our whole selves. Even divine revelation is subject to what Jonathan Edwards called the "affections." Our affections are what initially make us want to embrace or reject whatever we encounter, whether that thing is divine or not.[3] Our affections are also our initial tool for interpreting divine revelation. Part of navigating toward an authentic and articulate way of sharing our faith is recognizing the influence of our affections. By being aware of them, we can differentiate between what we believe God's message is and our interpretation of it.

Recognizing our affections also gives us insight into why we align ourselves with specific theological traditions. We select certain traditions to organize our beliefs less as a result of rational reflection and more because certain opinions about how to understand the Christian Tradition feel right to us. The combination of our affections with a theological tradition forms an interpretive matrix for how we approach divine revelation.

Our interpretive matrix can even influence which sources we accept as divine revelation. The kind of sources we choose—or that we simply rely on without thinking about it—speak to the kind of information that fits best with our image of God. Are there common, predominating themes in the sources we find most compelling? What are they? Do they point to specific

---

[3]Edwards differentiates between generic inclinations of people for or against something (whether we like or dislike it) with affections, which are more vigorous (whether we love or hate it). He also separates affections from passions, with the latter focusing more on animal instincts and involving less mental work. I use "affections" here because theological reflection should involve discovering what we feel most deeply about our beliefs. Jonathan Edwards, *A Treatise Concerning Religious Affections in Three Parts*, ed. John E. Smith (New Haven, CT: Yale University Press, 1959), 96-99.

character traits, activities or requirements of God? These are clues to the chief filters in our interpretive matrix.

Once we get a sense for why we have selected certain sources as revelation, we can further identify how our interpretive matrix works by considering how we weigh the material in those sources. How do we determine which portions of the sources come to the fore and help us make sense of the others? Many Christians, for example, would argue that the life and teachings of Jesus in the New Testament provide necessary insight into the Old Testament. Even though Old Testament prophets would not have known about Jesus of Nazareth when they prophesied about a coming redeemer, Christians hold that the revelation of the New Testament clarifies and explains what God was saying through the prophets. This is an interpretive move that is informed by our affections (it feels right) but also by several theological traditions that argue that Jesus is the center point for everything else in the Bible.

This example of reading the Old Testament in light of the New Testament assumes that the entire Bible has some level of authority. Not all theological traditions interpret the Bible this way. It is possible for someone to disagree with or even discount sections of a source that he or she might otherwise view as divine revelation. For example, certain feminist theological traditions criticize the book of Hosea because of the severe language it uses to describe how Hosea will punish his wife for her adultery. These traditions are not necessarily rejecting the Bible as divine revelation but are stating that part of the Bible runs counter to what they understand the nature and will of God to be. Therefore, they reject this specific part of the Bible as revelatory. Again, we would be likely to choose such an interpretation more because of our affections than because we have adopted a certain theological tradition.

Other theological traditions may not reject parts of a larger revelatory source outright but push for a reading of the text that is not self-evident. Christians who feel that drinking alcohol is sinful offer a good example here. Someone might point out that the Bible contains several passages that speak positively about wine (though not drunkenness) and that the Bible refers to Jesus drinking wine. Based on their affective distaste for alcohol combined with their theological tradition, these Christians would contend that the Bible is not referring to wine as we understand it today but to non-intoxicating grape juice. Therefore, when Jesus drank wine with his disciples at the Last Supper, he and his disciples were really sharing a common cup of grape juice. These Christians do not deny the authority of the Bible but argue that the plain reading of the word "wine" is corrupt and should be retranslated to "grape juice."

This is the power of the interpretive matrix. It sways us in what we believe God has revealed by interpreting those revelations in specific ways. In doing this it can create a self-reinforcing cycle for how we understand God. Our interpretive matrix influences us to assign the status of divine revelation to sources that agree with what we already feel God should say and do. When we read those sources, our matrix draws us to passages that affirm our interpretation. As a result we become more committed to our matrix.

If you sense a possible chicken-and-egg situation here (which comes first: The matrix we use to interpret revelation or the revelation we use to inform our matrix?), you are correct. What we bring to divine revelation tends to be what we take away from it. It is the existence of this cycle that demands that we become self-aware about our affections and the theological traditions we espouse. If we are unaware of the lens we use to receive information about God, we falsely believe we are encountering God's revelation without any interpretive bias. This blind spot puts us in a similar position to well-meaning evangelists and missionaries who dedicate their lives to spreading the gospel but do it as agents of social, political and economic forces. Their assumptions about what God wants people to be like are intertwined with their social, political and economic opinions, often without their realizing it. In the worst cases, the conflation of these opinions with the good news has led to imperialistic evangelists demanding adherence to their various assumptions as part of becoming a follower of Jesus Christ.

Becoming aware of our interpretive matrix also gives us the opportunity to change it. We do not need to be locked into a cycle of self-reinforcing beliefs. As we step back to consider why we believe what we do, we may conclude that we have confused certain agendas with the good news of God or allowed our affective likes and dislikes to define God's nature. If we recognize this, we can change it. This is not an easy process, but it is part of the formation that navigating evangelism requires. It also leads us to greater authenticity as we claim our affections and preferred theological traditions openly rather than making use of them without reflection.

In addition to making us more aware of how we interpret divine revelation, theological reflection can also give us insight into the interpretive matrices used by others. This is helpful in two ways vis-à-vis evangelism. First, it gives us greater insight into the evangelism resources we consult. These resources often offer packaged ideas for how evangelism should be understood, articulated and practiced. If we can determine the theological traditions, if not the affections, that influenced the authors of a resource, we can understand why that resource presents evangelism as it does. This will help us determine if we can accept the resource and its practices as an authentic reflection of what we believe. Second, by recognizing the complexities of how we interpret divine revelation, we can begin to appreciate other people's interpretations. This appreciation can help us move toward reconciliation across the theological traditions within the Christian family.

DIFFERENCES AND RECONCILIATION

History shows that theological disagreements are not an aberration in the church. These differences are often a result of different interpretations of divine revelation, which Christians have experienced since the book of Acts.

Rather than succumbing to anger and factionalism as a result of these disagreements, we are called to practice reconciliation within the church. This reconciliation is not about resolving specific disagreements (e.g., making conservatives and liberals agree) but living together within the Christian faith so that we maintain a unified community even when we disagree with each other.

At the outset, evangelism might seem like the last place we should look for support in the practice of reconciliation. Evangelism is a bias, and biases are usually a breeding ground for dissension rather than brotherly love! However, if we are serious about being the body of Christ, engaging in theological reflection together helps us find points of agreement we might not have acknowledged otherwise. It enables us to dig underneath our interpretations to find commonality in the Christian Tradition we all share. Let me offer an example with the three questions that are at the heart of theology.

Who is God? It would fall entirely outside of the Christian faith for someone to claim that God is wicked. This means that all theological traditions can agree that God is good.

What does God do? Theological traditions have another point in common here. Christians believe not only that God is good but that God does good things. It would even be fair to say that all Christians believe God desires people to share in God's goodness.

How do we respond to God? Given our common agreement that God is good and that God desires for people to share in God's goodness, all Christians can affirm that God desires humans to respond by participating in that goodness.

These are very basic points of agreement, and it is possible to move in different theological directions from them. Some of us might define the good God shares with people as deliverance from oppressive forces in this world, while others might define it as eternal life in heaven. Likewise, we could differ on what we think it means to participate in God's goodness. We could argue that it entails living in solidarity with and advocating for the poor, or that it is inviting people to pray to receive Jesus as their personal Lord and Savior, or that it means living by a rule of faith that allows the world to see the kind of alternative community the church can be.

Without trying to minimize these differences, consider how powerful it would be if all Christians started by recognizing that all other Christians believe that God is good and God wants to share that goodness with others. If we could accept this, it would foster a practice of reconciliation within the church. Those of us with different theological traditions would not see one another as competitors but as people who commonly desire to share God's goodness.

In recognizing this unified wish to invite people into God's goodness, we will find that many of our differences are complementary. Living in solidarity with the poor, offering people the chance to receive Jesus as Lord and Savior, and living according to a rule of life, for example, are not mutually exclusive. A person could engage in all three of these activities. Certainly an entire community of Christians could do all three. And even if a person or community were drawn to only one of these, it would not preclude that individual or community from recognizing the benefit of other Christians accomplishing the other two. The person living among the poor, the person inviting people to receive Jesus and the person living according to an alternative Christian ethic in a Christian community are all seeking to increase the access of people to God's goodness. They can support, pray for and see each other as part of a common mission rather than as adversaries who must be overcome.

Rick Richardson, an evangelism scholar who epitomizes the practice of reconciliation in his own life, has explored this reconciling potential of evangelism.[4] He explains how evangelism models drawn from a variety of theological traditions offer Christians the stepping stones to integration and synthesis rather than enmity.

Richardson describes seven models of evangelism: (1) evangelism as the public proclamation of the gospel, (2) evangelism as the conversion of individuals to the Christian faith, (3) evangelism as recruiting and making disciples of Jesus, (4) evangelism as church growth and planting, (5) evangelism as public acts of mercy, justice and peace, (6) evangelism as the distinctive life of an alternative community and (7) evangelism as the demonstration of God's power.

Each of these models is associated with one or more theological traditions. The first two are often associated with evangelicalism because of their emphasis on calling people to make a personal decision about their relationship with Jesus Christ. The third comes from a Wesleyan tradition with its emphasis on the need to grow continually in the grace of God. The fourth draws from a congregational tradition, focusing on the specific growth and development of individual congregations. The fifth is associated with the various liberation and postcolonial theologies that point to the privileged place the poor and marginalized have in God's will and the need to overcome oppressive social structures. The sixth could hail from an Anabaptist or Eastern Orthodox tradition, each of which emphasizes the uniqueness of the church ethically from the world around it. The seventh is Pentecostal with its focus on the supernatural power revealed by God through the Holy Spirit.

After surveying these models of evangelism, Richardson points to their positives and negatives. Each is well-suited to invite people into a part of God's goodness, but none is capable of ushering people fully into that goodness. His conclusion is that we should accept and support all of them, synthesizing them into forms of evangelism that offer as much of God's

---

[4]Richardson is an evangelical who is ordained as an Episcopalian priest and who annually ministers to attendees at the Burning Man festival in Nevada.

goodness to others as is humanly possible. I would add that where resources are lacking such that we are not able to synthesize all of these models, we should at least recognize the benefits and limitations of the evangelistic work we are doing. We can then gratefully acknowledge other expressions of God's goodness being manifested by Christians who operate out of a different theological tradition.

Theological reflection as part of navigating evangelism will not stop us from disagreeing with one another in the church, but it can help us appreciate the evangelistic power of one another's perspectives. If we have already accepted that all Christians start from a belief in the goodness of God's nature and God's activities, then it is possible for us to work alongside each other to share God's good news with the world.

Consider the benefits of even a marginally more unified church. It would allow us to allocate resources toward presenting the love of God in the world instead of using them to deal with intrachurch political squabbles. It would better demonstrate to those outside the church what the goodness of God looks like by the church living as a community of faith in which everyone is loved and respected even though we do not always agree. It would also allow the church to support a variety of evangelism practices that could appeal to a more diverse set of people.

Evangelism brings the good news to those within the church as much as it does to those outside of it. The best evangelists navigate evangelism not to establish their own unassailable beliefs but with the desire to be formed as they learn how to articulate the Christian Tradition for themselves and also to listen to others articulate their faith.

EVANGELISM AND THEOLOGICAL REFLECTION

A friend of mine once sent me a cartoon that depicted Jesus preaching the Sermon on the Mount. Instead of the Beatitudes, though, Jesus was delivering John Wesley's sermon on the Scripture way of salvation. The people around him were bewildered by his exposition on prevenient grace, with question marks surrounding their heads. This cartoon raises a good question we should ask before leaving this chapter: Is all this theological reflection necessary for evangelism? Can't we just share Jesus without all the formal theology? Wouldn't all this theology confuse those we want to reach?

Evangelism can be a simple conversation with someone about our belief in the good news. Hauling out our entire theological reasoning during that conversation likely would be off-putting to many people. However, this does not mean we can neglect theological reflection when we are navigating evangelism.

Just because we do not hear the concert pianist play the scales during a performance does not mean she avoids doing this work behind the scenes. Without it she would be less capable of presenting what we do hear when she is on stage. In the same way, if we do not invest the time and energy necessary to clarify what we believe and why we believe it, we will not be able to share our message of the good news as well as we could. The difference is that, for the pianist, the public performance presents the most complex pieces she can play. For us as evangelists, our public proclamation of the good news should be in the simplest words we can offer. The pianist practices the simple to share the complex. We reflect on the complex to offer the simple good news.

Such complex work is necessary because we tend to accrue our beliefs informally and inconsistently without intentional theological reflection. This is often referred to in theological education as "folk theology." Folk theology is by no means bad, but it tends to be disjointed. We may pick up some ideas about God from a prayer our grandmother said years before, from a bit of movie that seemed to explain something about the way the world works, from the lyrics to a song (regardless of whether than song was "Christian" or not) and from an anecdote in a sermon. There is no rhyme or reason to these sources, nor are they organized by any sort of tradition; they just individually resonated with us.

Folk theology without theological reflection is often on display at funerals. People who are broadly convinced that God's goodness extends to those who have died but who have not reflected theologically on that vague notion end up saying things that can be insensitive and harmful. Comments like "God just wanted another rose in his garden" may be well-intended and gesture toward the ultimate good God wants to bring about by caring for people after death, but they are also ill-informed and demonstrate a lack of understanding as to what the Christian Tradition teaches. This particular comment suggests that, in God's eyes, humans are little more than ornaments to adorn heaven. God is justified in gathering any human for this ornamental purpose at any time regardless of that person's age, station in life or relationships with others. The result is to make God out to be capricious, using divine power to bring death to those who might best beautify God's dwelling place. It is unlikely the person who said this actually believes these things, but it demonstrates how folk theology without theological reflection can lead to serious problems.

On the positive end, folk theology shows that we are paying attention to God. If we didn't care about God or ultimate things, we would not bother to gather ideas about the divine. We just need to improve on this process by putting time and energy into developing a coherent way of thinking about those eclectic ideas. This will translate into a more compelling way to articulate the good news both as individuals and as the church.

Navigating evangelism through theological reflection is both arduous and rewarding. It forces us to maneuver around and through our most basic assumptions about God and God's activities. In doing this we gain a greater capacity to explain our authentic faith, what we believe and why we believe it. We recognize the course we have chosen through the Christian Tradition by claiming our interpretive matrix, made of our gut-level affections and specific theological traditions. This includes reckoning with what we count as revelation and how we make sense of it. In short, this part of navigating evangelism leads us to self-awareness about our faith.

This self-awareness is not the only kind of awareness we need as we navigate evangelism, however. We also must be aware of other forces that shape us. We will address this in the next chapter.

Chapter Four

Putting the Good
News in Context

*R*everend Benkonda had worked for months to make this day happen.[1] An overworked pastor of five rural churches in the interior of Jamaica, Benkonda had a vision for holding a major evangelistic outreach in his largest church. He wanted this event to be moving and powerful, inviting the many unchurched people who lived nearby into a saving relationship with Jesus Christ.

I first learned of this when he made contact with a youth team I was a part of. He asked if we would support him by leading children's ministries during the week prior to the big evangelistic service and then participate in the service itself. He explained to us that the people would be more likely to attend the event if they knew Americans were helping lead it. We readily agreed and raised the money to go to Jamaica.

Impressive as bringing an American team to Jamaica was, Reverend Benkonda's greatest coup was securing a movie projector and an evangelistic film. The film shared the story of a young man who left a life of street gangs, violence and immorality when he repented and became a follower of Jesus Christ. Reverend Benkonda's church was located in a place known for fighting that often spilled into the streets, so he hoped the movie would resonate with the people. He planned to show the movie on the last night of the outreach, serving as the crescendo that would draw people forward to accept Christ.

After months of preparation and a week of our team running a vacation Bible school for the children in the community, the big day came. Our team

---

[1]This is a true story, but I have changed the pastor's name.

had generated good buzz by relating well to the children, so a large crowd showed up at the church. We started the service with some songs and short testimonies. The people from the neighborhood listened with interest. Reverend Benkonda's plan seemed to be coming together perfectly. Then came the high point as the lights were dimmed and the film began to play. The pastor watched in anticipation as the movie reenacted a major gang fight that would lead to the protagonist's conversion. He wondered if it would strike a chord with the people in attendance.

It did. The people burst into laughter. For those who lived facing the threats of real street violence, the stylized and sanitized depiction of violence presented in the movie was absurd at best. With that, all the effort Reverend Benkonda had put into the night was lost. The audience couldn't take anything else seriously, including the invitation to follow Jesus. Months of hoping, dreaming, planning and hard work by people from two nations collapsed.

After years of ministering in difficult circumstances, Reverend Benkonda knew what he believed about the good news of God. Seeing the poverty and violence surrounding him, he was convinced he had a better way for the people in the name of Jesus Christ. He also knew why he believed this, holding firmly to the Bible as God's divine revelation and interpreting that revelation through a lens of redeeming people from the low expectations and brokenness prevalent in their communities.

Reverend Benkonda's evangelism did not fail because his starting point was too small or his theological reflection was too shallow. It did not even fail because he did not understand the people he hoped to evangelize. It failed because he did not consider how the people in his Jamaican neighborhood would receive a film produced to meet the sensibilities of middle-class, evangelical, white Americans. The social and cultural differences were too much of a stretch for it to connect with the people in his church.

As we navigate our way from discerning our beliefs to developing an authentic understanding and practice of evangelism, we need to chart a course that makes us aware of our context and its impact on us. Just as a ship can pass only through channels that are deep and wide enough, so our beliefs and practices are shaped by the contexts in which we live. We need to map these contextual influences so we recognize their effects.

In addition, we need to be aware of how context shapes those with whom we want to share the good news. As the story of Reverend Benkonda demonstrates, if we fail to see how our own context connects or disconnects with the context of those we evangelize, our evangelism can fall flat.

INDIVIDUAL, CULTURE, SOCIETY AND COMMUNITY

Context is pervasive, unbidden and formative. This can make it difficult to analyze. Mark Lau Branson and Juan F. Martínez help us by providing a four-part schema of the contextual forces that shape us. These four parts are the individual, the culture, the society and the community. We will use this map of context as we navigate our way through these waters.

Individual. Context shapes us mostly through our interactions with other people. However, before we look at those interactions, we need to consider what we bring to them: our unique identities as individuals. We have already touched on this in describing the affections in the previous chapter. We can expand on that.

Each of us is a unique individual with value and dignity. We have remarkable powers of thought, reason, perception and creativity. We also have personalities, emotions, likes and dislikes, and a battery of other qualities that inform how we relate to the world around us and identify us as the specific individuals who are doing the relating. An array of diagnostic tools, such as the Myers-Briggs Type Indicator, help us label these traits.

On an intuitive level it is easy to recognize how multifaceted we are as individuals. Another person could know everything about when, where and how we grew into adulthood, and that person would still not fully know us. This is because each of us is more than the sum of the external influences that shaped us.

The number of academic disciplines dedicated to helping us understand ourselves as individuals—such as psychology, psychiatry, counseling and medicine—are a testament to this. These disciplines recognize that our mental, physical and relational well-being all play a role in how we think, act and relate to our context.

As evangelists, we must be aware of our individual proclivities. For example, if we are naturally introverted, we would be wise to develop evangelistic practices that do not require us to spend lots of time in large crowds.

Instead, we could focus on praying for those we hope will accept the good news and meet with people individually for conversation about faith at the local restaurant. If we suffer from hypertension, we would do better to order something other than coffee when we talk to those individuals.

Our evangelism is also improved if, insofar as we can, we get to know each person with whom we seek to share the good news. Becoming familiar with a specific context does not mean that we are prepared to share the gospel meaningfully with every individual in that context. People are not robots hardwired to respond to stimuli apart from their personal thoughts and feelings. As individuals we are capable of interpreting what we encounter and acting in ways that are surprising and unexpected. The more we know individuals, the more meaningfully we can share the good news.

All of this is messy and time-consuming. However, it is unavoidable. Evangelism is not just about spreading the message; it is about inviting people to be transformed by that message. This transformation is possible only if we as evangelists take stock of ourselves as individuals and engage with other people as individuals. To navigate evangelism well, we must look outward toward others, not just inward toward our own beliefs.

Not everything can be subsumed to the individual level, though. There are larger forces that form us, governing how individuals relate to one another and to the world around them. These are culture, society and community.

Culture. Culture, according to Branson and Martínez, "embodies patterned meanings that have been developed over time and are transmissible" to those who enter the culture either through birth or travel.[2] These patterned meanings include values and practices common to a group of people. In addition to these intangibles, culture also entails physical items that a group of people find commonly useful or meaningful.

Bathrooms offer a clear example of how culture operates in daily life. As anyone who has traveled to other cultures can attest, toilets (a physical item that is commonly useful within a culture) can vary greatly—from holes in the ground to elaborate seats reminiscent of starship captain chairs. Likewise, the process of cleansing after using the toilet (a commonly accepted practice

---

[2]Mark Lau Branson and Juan F. Martínez, *Churches, Cultures and Leadership* (Downers Grove, IL: IVP Academic, 2011), 80.

within a culture) is equally varied, from the use of hoses attached to the side of the toilet to toilet paper to plant leaves. These physical items (toilets) and practices (cleansing) represent common values about hygiene, cleanliness and comfort. An American's values would likely be transgressed when asked to use a hose to rinse off in a Burmese bathroom without any soap or towel provided, just as a Burmese person would be shocked at being told to put their hand in a certain place to use toilet paper.

Cultures tend to develop among people who share a common identity. Usually we think of this common identity among people who live in a similar geographical area. This is why it does not surprise us to encounter different cultures when we travel outside of the geographical area we usually inhabit.

But cultures can also develop among people who have other reasons to claim a common identity. People who share an ethnic heritage (such as immigrants in a foreign country) or who are approximately the same age (such as Gen-Xers, millennials and other generational groups) are groups with common identities that can lead to distinct cultures. This means there can be cultures within cultures. For example, a group of second-generation immigrants to the United States might be negotiating three sets of cultures: the mainstream culture in the country where they live, the culture of the nation their parents emigrated from and the culture developed within their age group.

As evangelists we need to be sensitive to how people relate to the cultures and cultures within cultures around them. This will allow us to demonstrate connections between the good news of God and the values and practices that these cultures already accept.

Recognizing that many people are operating under the influence of more than one culture also allows us to be agents of peace. People who relate to multiple cultures can be placed in wrenching situations when those cultures conflict. We have the opportunity in these situations to offer the good news as a metanarrative of peace that overarches these competing voices. We should be careful not to offer the good news as one more voice that demands allegiance.

When people move across cultures, culture shock is frequently a result. Culture shock upends cultural assumptions about how to engage in certain practices or to use certain physical things. According to cultural communication specialist Gary Weaver, people rely on certain cues for how to act.

These cues are culturally defined and prompt specific responses.[3] When someone enters a new culture, the cues may be entirely different, so that person does not know how to respond. Or the cues may be the same but the expected responses are different. For example, when people meet for the first time (a cue), in some cultures the expected response is a handshake whereas in others it is a bow. This loss of familiar cues and responses can lead to a breakdown in communication and, in severe situations, an identity crisis in the person encountering the new culture. Overcoming culture shock requires the person being introduced to the new culture to become aware of his or her preconceived cultural assumptions and to learn the new cultural values, practices and use of things.

Our responsibility as evangelists is to be as attentive as possible in moving across cultures. We must be aware, or at least become aware, of our own cultural assumptions. It is not wrong for us to have these assumptions— all people have them—but it is wrong to become chauvinistic about them, declaring other cultures to be deficient or evil because of their different cues and responses.

Even more dangerous than claiming cultural superiority is an inability to separate our cultural assumptions from the good news we seek to share. The failure of evangelists on this point stands at the heart of most postcolonial critiques of evangelism and missionary work. Since culture imparts basic assumptions people hold about the world, it also influences how people think about God, the way God acts, and how people are to respond to God. This means that theology, and even the way people understand the good news, is culturally patterned.

The cultural formation of our beliefs is not bad; it is a given. Recognizing this, we must be open to communicating the good news in different ways, especially if we are moving across cultures when we share it. We may continue to hold to the cultural manifestations of the good news that are meaningful to us, but we must also be willing to see the good news become manifest in other cultures in unexpected ways. We need to undertake this process whether we are missionaries going to a new country or middle-aged

---

[3]Weaver's entire theory about culture shock and how to deal with it can be found in Gary R. Weaver, "Understanding and Coping with Cross-Cultural Adjustment Stress," in *Education for the Intercultural Experience*, ed. R. Michael Paige (Yarmouth, ME: Intercultural Press, 1993), 137-67.

people working with a local youth group. In each case we are called to recalibrate our cultural expectations concerning how the good news becomes a reality in people's lives.

Society. Society refers to the structures a group develops to order its life. This is why certain terms are prefaced by "socio-," such as sociopolitical or socioeconomic. These refer to structures of governance and commerce that pervade how people relate to one another.

Usually society operates according to cultural norms, but it can take on a life of its own when the structures become more powerful. Anyone who has entered the legal, corporate, governmental, financial or ecclesiastical arenas quickly becomes aware of rules within these structures that stretch and modify the common cultural practices. Entering into these structures requires more than just an open mind culturally; it requires an orientation in the unique vocabularies, traditions, rituals and objects each social structure uses.

Beyond ordering daily life, social structures also mediate major life transitions. This makes it incumbent on evangelists, and any sort of minister, to learn these social structures well. For example, a pastor must be familiar not only with the cultural norms surrounding death and marriage but also with the legal issues associated with each. If the pastor officiates at a wedding but never signs or returns the marriage license issued by the local government, then the pastor has failed to legalize the marriage and potentially committed a crime. Likewise, a pastor who understands how to visit with a bereaved family but who does not know what a funeral home does or how payment for funerals is arranged may end up in an awkward situation if looked to for guidance by the family.

As evangelists we must look for interpreters who can help us understand these social structures. A person in local ministry, such as the pastor of a congregation, often has these sorts of interpreters immediately available in the congregation. However, it still takes an intentional effort on the part of the pastor to connect with and learn from these interpreters. Those of us who are not in local church pastorates need to find interpreters by building relationships with people in various social structures. This often requires getting to know people in the institutions that maintain these structures. By knowing the social structures that define important daily patterns of life for a group of people, we are better equipped to share the good news with those people in a meaningful way.

Community. The community, according to Branson and Martínez, is a more intimate grouping of people that operates within larger cultures and social structures. Unlike cultures and societies, communities are not entities to which individuals are automatically connected. People voluntarily join communities because they find the purposes, values, beliefs, activities or other characteristics of these groups meaningful. A community is made up of individuals who have a "shared hope and imagination" and often cooperate in "side-by-side activities rooted in shared meanings and goals."[4]

While cultures and social structures impose formation on people, communities give individuals a chance to select specific contours of their formation. At minimum, a community allows people to relate to others who share a common interest (such as a bowling league). At most, communities encourage their members to claim a common metanarrative (such as, in the most extreme case, a cult). Regardless of how extensive the community's demands on an individual are, the community offers a means for the individual to be formed in ways that the culture and society do not.

The community not only offers a different kind of formation than the culture and the society; it has the potential to help the individual resist the formation of the culture and the society. This is because a community can provide individuals with an alternative set of values than those imposed by the culture and society.

Alasdair MacIntyre argues that a community has the capacity to deem people virtuous who hold fast to its identity in the face of pressure to let go of it.[5] Often this pressure is brought to bear by people who want to bring those in the community into conformity with cultural and social norms. Driven by the desire to be virtuous, members of a community may persevere under such pressure. They may even be able to critique the culture and society in return.

Branson and Martínez place the local congregation into the category of community. This means that a congregation must negotiate cultural, social and community values, especially if it wants to be evangelistic. As

---

[4]Branson and Martínez, *Churches, Cultures and Leadership*, 83.
[5]MacIntyre, *After Virtue*, 126-27.

a congregation navigates evangelism, it must map a route that stays true to the Christian identity while staying within the identified boundaries of culture and society when possible. If it strays too far out of the cultural and social channels, the good news it offers will be indecipherable to the people outside the community. Conversely, if it gives up its Christian identity to abide by the culture and society, it can lose its uniqueness and become little more than a chaplain that baptizes cultural and social values.[6]

The congregation's role in navigating the Christian identity through its cultural and social context raises another point about evangelism: A person who is evangelized needs to be invited into a community. Individuals can rarely enact the good news of God alone. They need a community of people who can provide support, encouragement, discipline, reproof and account- ability. Without this, the lures of individualism, cultural values and social convention can easily pull a person off course.[7] As John Wesley famously remarked, there is "no holiness but social holiness," meaning that it is virtually impossible for individuals to live a holy life apart from a community of faith.[8]

Individuals, cultures, societies and communities are all aspects of human existence that we must recognize as we navigate evangelism. We can do this by learning both how these forces have formed our lives and how they have formed those with whom we seek to share the good news. However, we must move beyond recognition to engagement. In the next section we will con- sider how to do this.

CREATIVE ENGAGEMENT

A potential danger in discussing culture and society in relation to evan- gelism is to make it sound like the church is locked in a zero-sum game with

---

[6]For an example of how an entire denomination chose the latter route in its attempt to negotiate its relationship to American culture, see Mark R. Teasdale, *Methodist Evangelism, American Salva- tion* (Eugene, OR: Pickwick, 2014).

[7]Andrew Walls, a famous missionary and missiologist, explains this in the poignant story of Thomas Tooi, a Maori warrior who became a convert to Christianity and lived two years with missionaries in Australia. He returned to New Zealand as a missionary to his own people but without any support from the missionaries who had nurtured his faith. Within weeks he lapsed into headhunting, cannibalism and other native activities. Walls concludes this cautionary tale by emphasizing the importance of converts being supported by a community of faith. Andrew Walls, *Cross-Cultural Process in Christian History: Studies in the Transmission and Appropriation of Faith* (Maryknoll, NY: Orbis, 2002), 11-12.

[8]John Wesley and Charles Wesley, *Hymns and Sacred Poems* (Bristol, England: Felix Farley, 1743), v.

its context. Either cultural values and social conventions will stand firm against the good news of Christ or the Christian faith will take hold and wipe out all cultural and social norms. Alternately, the good news and the cultural values could both be watered down to the point that they can co-exist but are no longer true to themselves.[9]

The problem with this zero-sum thinking is that culture and society are both pervasive, affecting all people, including Christians. There is nothing insidious about this. Even individuals who choose to participate in a community with a well-defined identity that resists cultural values are still part of the culture and society around them. A student of mine who was a pastor in the Upper Peninsula of Michigan, a place where residents proudly refer to themselves as "Yupers," put it this way: While the people in his congregation are committed to Jesus Christ, this does not stop the people from being Yupers. "By the time they reach my church door," he explained, "Yu-pification has already occurred." He is exactly right. His church attendees are simultaneously members of his congregation's faith community and Yupers who are well-versed in Yuper cultural values and social structures (like participation in the annual Humungus Fungus Fest in Crystal Falls). These claims on their identities are not exclusive. They sit side by side.

This more complex interrelationship among culture, society and community suggests that we must have a more complex set of tools for sharing the good news. Two authors, Lamin Sanneh and Andy Crouch, help us in developing these tools.

Internal formation: Lamin Sanneh. Lamin Sanneh is a missiologist who was born in The Gambia and converted in young adulthood from Islam to the Christian faith. In his book *Translating the Message: The Missionary Impact on Culture* he contends that the Christian faith is unique in its willingness to see the divine revelation presented in the Bible as translatable.[10] Translating

---

[9]There is an unfortunately long precedent for thinking about the relationship between the church and culture this way. As critics of H. Richard Niebuhr's classic *Christ and Culture* (New York: Harper & Row, 1975) have pointed out, while his typologies of the ways Christians relate to culture can be helpful, the text suffers from treating Christians and the church as entirely independent from culture. An excellent and easily accessible explanation of this critique is found in Andy Crouch, *Culture Making: Recovering Our Creative Calling* (Downers Grove, IL: InterVarsity Press, 2008), 178-83.

[10]Lamin Sanneh, *Translating the Message: The Missionary Impact on Culture*, rev. ed. (Maryknoll, NY: Orbis Books, 2009), 56.

the Bible into different languages that are bound by time and space does not remove the power of the good news that it bears but legitimizes the good news of Jesus Christ as being for all people in all places throughout all time. He contrasts this with the Islamic notion that the revelation of the Qur'an is properly available only through reading it in Arabic and can be obeyed only by adopting specific cultural values and social structures.[11]

Sanneh's claim that the good news of Jesus Christ is translatable without loss of meaning or power gets at the interweaving of culture, society and community by showing that the nature of the good news is to engage all levels of human existence. It invites not just individuals to share in God's goodness but entire cultures and social structures.

Sanneh connects these pieces even more helpfully when he describes a three-phase process through which the early Christian community forged its identity while learning to engage with the culture and society. These three phases are:

1. *Quarantine.* The community maintains strict boundaries between itself and the surrounding culture in order to develop its identity without being diluted by external influences.

2. *Syncretism.*[12] The community makes sense of how to be faithful to Jesus Christ as it interacts with the culture.

3. *Reform.* The community engages in prophetic and missionary activities to influence and even transform the culture with the Christian faith.[13]

While Sanneh presents these as a descriptive model, those of us who are in evangelistic communities today can use them as prescriptive, practicing each phase in turn. First, in order to maintain a clear identity that is formed out of the good news, we who are members of Christian communities must devote ourselves periodically to spending time only with one another and with God. Retreats and other times dedicated to spiritual practices and

---

[11]Ibid., 274-76.

[12]The word *syncretism* is often used to describe the negative influence of cultural and social forces on the Christian faith, warping the gospel. Sanneh shifts the locus of power in his use of the term, suggesting that it is the Christian community steeped in the gospel that is going out to engage the culture and society around them. Having firmly established themselves in the Christian identity, they do not fear being corrupted by this engagement.

[13]Ibid., 36-39.

retelling the good news that has been handed down to us through the Christian Tradition are essential to this. Entering into this quarantine serves a catechetical role, allowing us to learn (or relearn) the basic intellectual beliefs of the Christian faith as our communities teach them, to experience the presence of God and the support of our fellow community members and to be initiated into the central purposes and practices of our respective Christian communities.

The first two stages of navigating evangelism fit into this quarantine phase. Discerning the good news that serves as our starting point and reflecting on it theologically so we can articulate our authentic beliefs about God are essential to a Christian community's identity.

Once we have spent time in quarantine, we are equipped to face the rigors of integrating our cultural and social context into our faith. Initially this happens as we enter public settings of daily life. What does it mean to be a bearer of the good news of Jesus Christ in the marketplace, in the workplace, in school, in seminary? In many cases there may be no significant changes to how we act in these places (for example, our expectation about whether to shake hands or bow when meeting someone will not change). However, when we encounter the ethical questions of daily life, such as how to treat a beggar on the street or how to react to a public tragedy, we should find that our Christian identity informs us in ways that the culture and society do not.

As we act in accord with our Christian identity, we offer a witness to those around us for how someone can be part of the culture and the society while still being formed by the good news of Jesus Christ. This is potent enough if we live this way as individual members of the community. It is even more powerful if the community as a whole demonstrates consistency and authenticity in how its members live in the public eye.

This syncretism phase fits with the contextual stage of navigating evangelism. Once we have reached the point of articulating what we believe and why we believe it, we learn how to move smoothly through the specific groups of people and situations in which we must make those beliefs known.

When we have sufficiently integrated our cultural and social assumptions with our Christian identity, we are ready to reflect on the culture and society in light of the good news of God. We can offer insights into how the culture and society foster assumptions, practices and values that are destructive or unjust. We can also lift up those aspects of the culture and society that we believe are beneficial to people, drawing them toward the goodness we believe God desires for them. Again, this is not just a matter of individual prophets being raised up who will address the culture and society. It is the community of faith speaking to the culture and the society.

This last phase deals with the final stage of navigating evangelism: developing our evangelistic practices. With a clear sense of what we believe about God's goodness and how we can share our beliefs in a contextually meaningful way, we are ready to embody our authentically held beliefs in our words and actions.

What is compelling about Sanneh's model is that it allows us as individual evangelists and evangelistic communities to embrace the multiple forces that shape us. We do not have to reject our cultural and social formation. Rather, we incorporate them into our community identity, creating a faithful witness to the good news. It even points to Christian communities being strong enough to challenge and commend the culture and society.

Another strength of this model is that it re-equips the laity to do evangelism. For too long evangelism has been seen as the bailiwick of the professional evangelist who has been specially trained with the right words and techniques to convince people to become Christians. Taking the cultural, social and communal aspects of formation seriously moves us away from this sort of specialization.

The best evangelists are those who are connected to a Christian community and who are conversant with the cultural and social norms around them. Frequently, the laity is more capable of moving through the cultural practices and social structures than the clergy because the laity must interact with them in ways that many clergy—who are socialized into the peculiar structure of the church—never do. Laypeople are also more credible in their evangelism for this reason.[14] If they engage with the culture in a specific way because of their faith, it is clear they have a deep and authentic belief system out of which they operate. If clergy act in the same way, it is easier to chalk it up to their being somewhat alien to the culture and society at the outset.

---

[14]George Hunter has written extensively on the importance of credible laypeople to evangelize effectively. George G. Hunter III, "Apostolic Ministry Through an Empowered Laity," in *Radical Outreach: The Recovery of Apostolic Ministry and Evangelism* (Nashville: Abingdon, 2003), 97-118.

Having done this preparatory work of integrating our cultural and social formation into our identity as Christian communities, let us look more closely at Sanneh's reform phase, which claims that Christian communities can transform their contexts. As we saw at the beginning of this section, reformation should not fall into zero-sum thinking of just embracing or rejecting what culture and society have to offer. We need a more robust way of reforming our context. This is where Andy Crouch's book *Culture Making* is helpful.

Toward cultivation and creation. In his book, Crouch lays out a continuum of ways that Christians have related to culture, helpfully using words that all begin with the letter *c*.[15] In each case he describes the posture of Christians in relation to cultural products such as movies, media and other physical manifestation of the assumptions nested in culture. Tying in Branson and Martínez's ideas, I would suggest these also apply to how Christians relate to society.

1. *Condemn.* Christians reject the cultural or social product. This could involve boycotting a movie, passing church resolutions against a political or economic policy, or otherwise determining that culture and society have produced something entirely unacceptable to the Christian community.

2. *Critique.* Christians accept the product, but they believe it is flawed and must be rehabilitated. This is often a stance that Christians take toward government or corporate actions, believing, for example, that the basic social structures of democracy and capitalism are sound but that specific ways they are practiced must be reformed.

3. *Copy.* Christians believe that the form of the product is worthwhile, just not the content, so they develop their own versions of these products. Contemporary Christian music is an example of this, using the same styles of music that are on offer in the larger culture but with lyrics modified to fit the tastes of at least certain Christian communities.

4. *Consume.* Christians accept the products as they are. This could be because they have weighed the merits of the products or are simply

---

[15]Crouch, *Culture Making*, 78-100.

unreflectively accepting what is in front of them. Regardless, this activity ties Christians more closely to the cultural and social norms in which they live.

Crouch suggests that these can all be appropriate ways for Christians to relate to culture. However, he goes on to say that if Christians want to make a difference in the culture, these responses are not enough. These responses are all reactive, allowing others to take the initiative in shaping cultural norms and social structures. To reform the culture, Christians must take the lead by developing new products and practices that are for everyone. He offers two additional *c*'s to this end: create and cultivate.[16]

According to Crouch, culture does not change when people react to it but when current products, practices and assumptions are replaced with something new. Fortunately, this sort of cultural change takes place on a regular basis. If Christians create compelling products and practices that catch on with the general population, they can replace the existing ones and forge a new set of cultural values and social structures that are infused with the good news. This is hard work, and there are many pitfalls involved in trying to create popular cultural and social products (Crouch admits this).[17] But just as Hollywood and Madison Avenue find it worthwhile to endure many flops in order to create a few cultural hits, so the church should see the value in this work as well.

Crouch urges the church to cultivate space for this cultural creation just as the movie and advertising industries do. Imagine that incubators existed where Christians could go to dream and create cultural products and practices. The church could cultivate these spaces on local, regional, national and even international levels. Seminaries (literally, "seedbeds") would be especially well-positioned for this work.

The need for cultivation brings us back to Sanneh's three phases. In order to cultivate new cultural products and practices, members of a Christian community need to know their own core Christian identity as well as the culture and society in which they are set. Missing either of these pieces will cause the cultural products that Christians develop either to be too narrowly Christian to be of interest to those outside the Christian community or to

---

[16]Ibid., 65-77.
[17]Ibid., 193-95.

be too culturally conditioned to be recognizably Christian. If the community can find the right mixture, then its products and practices will be equally acceptable in the church and in the larger population. The hope is that as people in the larger population adopt these new creations, their values will shift toward the good news of God.

My own addition to Crouch's proposition is that the church might most profitably look at creating cultural practices that deal with problems the culture has not yet addressed well. There is ample room, for example, for the church to pioneer practices in how to relate to ex-offenders being released back into mainstream society, for providing practices of community development that reclaim neighborhoods blighted by poverty and violence, and for supporting families struggling with the demands of special-needs children. Almost anything that requires healing or caring for those on the margins of culture and society is ripe for new cultural practices and products. The church just needs to cultivate the space for its people to create these practices and products.

All of this bears directly on evangelism. In navigating evangelism, we first find our starting point, discerning the good news from which we will launch our evangelistic work. We then reflect theologically on that good news, becoming aware of what we believe about God and why we believe it. Recognizing that even our theological reflection is influenced by outside forces, we also work to become aware of our context. We take stock of our individual proclivities as well as of the culture, society and communities that surround us.

Recognizing our context, we then see that the power of evangelism is more than just inviting individuals to reconsider their identities in the light of the good news of Jesus Christ. It is also to sanctify the very forces that form individuals' values and assumptions. When we navigate evangelism, we should not see culture and society as rock walls hemming us in but as sandbars we sometimes avoid and sometimes dredge, transforming them into new channels for the good news of God to flow to people.

The practices of evangelism that we are navigating toward are much grander and more creative than we might have imagined at the outset of the journey. We can now begin to consider what these practices might be.

Chapter Five

Fashioning New Wineskins for the Old, Old Story

*E*vening had long since settled on the warm south Virginia countryside. Out in the hills, more than an hour away from the closest town, a men's retreat was in full swing. Rough voices, cracked with long dormant emotion, filled the air with old hymns. As the songs ended the voices shifted. Heavy sobs took the place of lyrics as the men were wracked with remorse over their sins and cried out for forgiveness. This contrition soon gave way to tears of joy as the retreat leader recalled them to the gracious nature of God. They rejoiced as they claimed the mercy of God through Jesus Christ in their own lives.

Emotion crackled throughout the room as the leader told the men to join in a group hug. The men willingly complied. Their defenses were down and they were grateful for an opportunity to share in closer fellowship with their brothers.

All except for me. Sitting near the back of the room, I had not experienced the emotional outburst the others had. It was not that I did not believe in God or was not grateful for the grace given through Jesus Christ, but I had not found the events of the evening so moving. Watching the men gather for their hug, I realized that the group would soon break for the evening and the men would head back to their rooms. This brought another thought to mind . . . Twinkies.

The retreat had an especially well-stocked snack table. The golden prize of the table, which always seemed to disappear before anything else, was the

Twinkies. I realized that I had been granted a few short minutes to make my way to the snack table in the next room while the other men were focused on their hug, guaranteeing that I would be able to claim a Twinkie for myself.

With the men distracted, I quietly made my way through the door and over to the snack room. I congratulated myself on my strategy and reached toward the newly restocked pile of Twinkies with glee.

Before I could grasp my reward, however, I felt my feet leave the floor as I was hoisted into the embrace of a much larger, much stronger man. One of the retreat leaders had noticed my departure and followed me into the snack room. When I was preoccupied with Twinkies, this huge man grabbed me in a bear hug, lifting me into the air and rendering me immobile.

In a voice strained with emotion, the leader admonished me for my carnal thoughts during this spiritual time. He pled with me to give up my sin and declare my love for Jesus. He stated emphatically that he would not let me go until I confessed that love.

Alarmed by my situation, I managed to say a few words about my belief that the leader evidently found acceptable. Released from his grip, I hastily made my way back to my cot for the night, leaving the Twinkies undisturbed.

The leader had a legitimate point about my lack of support for my brothers in Christ even if I was not experiencing the emotions they were. However, it was my extreme discomfort during his evangelizing of me that has always stuck in my memory. This experience stands as a constant reminder to me that the final test of evangelism is how we practice it. We can be articulate in our beliefs about the good news, theologically astute about what we believe and contextually sensitive, but if our practices fail to extend that good news in a way that others can receive it, our entire enterprise collapses. We will have navigated our evangelism onto the rocks.

This last stage of navigation requires us to maneuver through two challenges: creativity and change. Creativity deals with adapting our beliefs to practice; change deals with modifying our existing practices. We will look at each in turn.

CREATIVITY

Evangelistic practices are not just means to advance a specific message; they are manifestations of the actual good news. The practices we develop should flow naturally from what we claim the good news to be. This is why creativity is so important. We need the new wineskins of new practices to hold the good news we have come to articulate. Cramming our authentic beliefs into old practices that do not flow from our beliefs will leave us burned out and disillusioned, convinced that evangelism is not something we are equipped to do.

Sadly, it's common for us as Christians to use practices that do not demonstrate what we believe the good news to be. This is especially visible in local churches struggling to buck a downward trend in their membership numbers. In these cases the churches lose sight of their starting point as they try to stay afloat. Desperate for anything that might save them, they grab at evangelism programs, form evangelism committees and try all manner of gimmicks to attract new parishioners. The results are predictable. Motivated by a fear of death rather than the good news that excites them about believing in God through Jesus Christ, their efforts yield little beyond their own exhaustion.

This is not to condemn these congregations or the hardworking, well-meaning people who want to see them thrive (I have served in some of these churches!). It is to point out that our evangelism will be ineffective when we fail to be creative enough to develop practices that are motivated by what we authentically believe is the good news.

Individuals can fall into the same trap. Having few examples to draw from other than famous evangelists, individual Christians often feel stuck when it comes to their own personal efforts. They know how they have seen evangelism practiced, but they have difficulty connecting that practice to their own understanding of the good news. Here the issue is not that these individuals have lost sight of their starting point but that they cannot reconcile incarnating the good news they believe in with the specific practices they think are acceptable as evangelism.

When we have come so far in the work of navigating evangelism, it is frustrating to be stymied at this point. To get over this hump, it helps to remember the first point from chapter one: We need to expand our understanding of what evangelism is. In navigating evangelism we begin by overcoming the stereotypes of what an evangelist looks like. Then we expand our understanding of evangelism to make room for starting points and theological traditions that are not usually connected to evangelism. Now we need to finish this work by creatively developing practices of evangelism that we may never have thought of as being evangelistic. Any practice that embodies the good news can properly be named evangelistic.

Fortunately, to be creative does not require us to generate our practice from nothing. Both the Bible and the lives of the saints offer us examples of activities we may never have thought of as evangelistic.

In the Bible we return to the Great Commission (Mt 28:16-20). The passage begins with disciples of varying commitment levels arriving to meet with Jesus. After the disciples arrive, they worship. They are called into the presence of Jesus before Jesus sends them to others. An important practice of evangelism, then, is spending time in the presence of Jesus.

It is after this time of worship that Jesus commissions the disciples. He does not commission them to convert people but to engage with others in multifaceted ways. The disciples are to "go" (a verb that does not mean for the disciples to "get away from here" but to live their faith as they move through their daily lives). As they go, they are to make new disciples. They do this by baptizing them into the Christian community and teaching them to live according to the ways Jesus taught.

There are three lessons about evangelistic practices in this commission. First, evangelism encompasses multiple activities. Second, the activities

LEARNING ACTIVITY

There are many magazines, videos and texts available offering evangelism advice, products and services to local congregations and individual Christians. These materials base their recommended practices on techniques from the marketing world, strategies from large churches and the experiences of individual evangelists, arguing that these practices are the most effective in attracting new members and converts. However, these materials rarely invite us to consider why we should engage in these practices or if the practices fit with our authentic beliefs. Taking time to examine these materials carefully and reflect on whether the practices they promote work alongside our beliefs can help us determine which activities we should pursue.

that Jesus commissions his disciples to undertake are about relationship, not revivalism. The disciples will meet people as they go about their lives, invite them to participate in the community of faith, and initiate them as new disciples within that community. Third, the entire community shares the relational work of evangelism. While individual disciples will encounter those outside the community, the community as a whole undertakes the process of forming people as new disciples. The community does this in a way that looks more like an apprentice model than a model that pushes for a person to make an immediate decision to convert. New disciples are coached over time how to obey the teachings of Jesus within the community.

These three lessons are enough to show us that the practice of evangelism makes room for a variety of activities that elude our stereotypes. Strengthening this point are the many other passages that deal with evangelism in the Bible. The other four postresurrection commissioning passages, for example, list activities beyond what we find in the Matthew passage. These include healing the sick, exorcising demons and offering peace.

Along with the Bible, we have the examples of the saints to help us practice evangelism creatively. A survey of the evangelistic activities of just a few saints demonstrates the creative ways Christians can share the good news. There are the wonder-working evangelists like Martin of Tours and Gregory Thaumaturgus. There are the evangelists who practiced a form of early ethnography, like Patrick and Boniface. There are the peacemakers like Francis of Assisi when he sought to end the Crusades by gaining an audience with the Sultan. There are the monastics and mystics like Julian of Norwich, Teresa of Ávila, John of the Cross and Ignatius of Loyola. There are those concerned with the plight of the needy like John Chrysostom, Bartolomé de las Casas and Mary McLeod Bethune. There are powerful orators like George Whitefield, Jarena Lee and Charles Finney. There are the organizers like John Wesley, Jennie C. Hartzell, William Wadé Harris and John R. Mott. There are scholars like Jonathan Edwards and Helen Barrett Montgomery. There are reformers like Martin Luther, John Calvin and the Grimké sisters. In addition to all of these, there are the Christians who have been our personal saints by how they have blessed our lives and so provided examples of how to bear the good news to others.

The saints provide us with at least two points in reference to evangelism. First, spiritual formation is a necessary practice for the evangelist. Just as the disciples needed to linger in the presence of Jesus before being commissioned, so the saints engaged in processes of discerning what they believed about God and disciplining their lives around those beliefs. To follow the evangelistic example of the saints, we must begin our evangelistic practice by looking to our formation in the faith.[1]

Second, we do not have to fit a specific theological or psychological profile to practice evangelism. Looking at the diversity of the saints, we find role models for how to practice evangelism regardless of the theological traditions we claim or personalities we have. We may even find their witness to the good news so compelling that we want to widen or modify our beliefs to include what they shared. Their creativity in articulating and embodying the good news should challenge us in our theological reflection as well as in our evangelistic practice.

Even if we do not want to imitate the saints, their array of practices demonstrates that Christians have successfully wedded their belief in the good news with creative evangelistic activities throughout history. Their examples offer us ideas for how we can make this connection and encouragement to do it well.

LEARNING ACTIVITY

Theological education often focuses on the failures of the Christian church, especially how Christians have abused power-supporting structures that protected the privileged and harmed the marginalized. These are important lessons that keep us humble about the church's role in history. But we should also learn about the times Christians got it right. We do have genuine heroes in the church. Learning about Christians from a variety of times and theological traditions who set good examples can help us find role models to follow as evangelists. It can also encourage us in our personal faith.

---

[1]This moves us toward spiritual formation. While spiritual formation is a distinct field of study from evangelism in the academy, the two cannot be separated from each other in how we practice evangelism. The Christian who does not strive after sanctification is a Christian who will struggle to navigate evangelism. For a text on spiritual formation that draws the same conclusion, see Gordon T. Smith, *Called to Be Saints: An Invitation to Christian Maturity* (Downers Grove, IL: InterVarsity Press, 2014).

Whether we draw from the Bible, the saints or anywhere else, the goal is to fire our imaginations so that we can be creative in developing our practices of evangelism. We are freed from the constraints of a reduced range of evangelistic activity. In this freedom we can let our practices flow creatively out of our authentic beliefs, embodying the good news that we treasure and would like others to receive.

One of the best ways to unleash this creativity is to make use of the experiences we have had being evangelized. Think about how the evangelist treated you and how you responded. If you could rewrite that moment of history, how would you improve on what happened? Take into account everything you have articulated about the good news through your theological reflection and contextual sensitivity in reimagining the scenario. Would the encounter have taken place in a different location? Would it have happened over several days, weeks or months rather than in a single setting? Would it have involved the evangelist speaking or acting differently? Would the message itself have been articulated differently?

As you answer these questions, draw from the examples of the Bible and the saints to develop practices you could use in other situations to share the good news. As you construct these, keep Jesus' admonition to do unto others as you would have done unto you in mind. Think about evangelistic practices that you would want to have practiced on you. If the practice is something that would convey God's goodness to you, it is likely that you will be able to enact it in a way that offers that goodness to someone else.

If we are developing these practices for a congregation, we should gather to share these scenarios with one another. In them we can hear what is important to each member of our community in how we convey the good news. This provides us with a foundation from which we can weave what excites us about the good news into ways we can practice evangelism together.

CHANGE

Finding a way to unlock our creativity in moving our beliefs from ideas to actions overcomes the first challenge. Putting our creative activities into practice is the second. New ideas and practices require changing from our old ways of thinking about and doing evangelism.

Most people become skittish when confronted with change, even when that change is clearly for the better. Robert Kegan and Lisa Laskow Lahey explain this behavior in their book *Immunity to Change*. They demonstrate that when people are faced with change they weigh four factors: (1) an explanation of why they need to change to honor a certain commitment, (2) a description of what they are currently doing or not doing that works against that change taking place, (3) other commitments they worry they won't be able to fulfill if the change occurs and (4) a "big assumption" they make that explains why they're safer if they don't change.[2] While the first two factors acknowledge there is good reason to change and recognize what hinders that change from happening, the authors argue that the strength of the last two factors always trumps these. As a result, we do not change.

This explains why we often resist adopting creative practices of evangelism. As individuals we may desire to share the good news, but we are concerned about coming across as hostile or unloving if we change how we speak or act toward the people around us. As congregations we may see the need for more creative ways to reach new people, but we struggle with the possibility that changing our way of reaching out to others will cause us to lose support from existing members. In each case we are caught between conflicting commitments: one that argues for change and one that militates against it.[3]

Kegan and Lahey use a series of columns based on four factors to help people see their conflicting commitments and practices. They call this an "immunity X-ray." Using the examples of the individual and the congregation in the above paragraph, let's see how this calculus works. First, the individual:

Commitment That Requires Change	Doing or Not Doing to Resist Change	Worries About Other Commitments	Big Assumption Against Change
Being convinced of the good news God offers in Jesus Christ for all people	Not sharing my faith publicly	Wanting to maintain good relationships with friends; not wanting to be a hypocrite by speaking up as a Christian who has obvious flaws on display	If I share about my faith, people will think that I am weird and potentially offensive, shutting down any hope of them taking the good news seriously

---

[2] Robert Kegan and Lisa Laskow Lahey, *Immunity to Change: How to Overcome It and Unlock Potential in Yourself and Your Organization* (Boston: Harvard Business Press, 2009), 227-51.
[3] Kegan and Lahey dedicate the entire second portion of their book to looking at how individuals and organizations can understand their respective immunities to change.

In this case, the change the individual is considering involves moving from not being publicly identified as a Christian to sharing their faith with others. The person is committed to this change because of how important the good news God offers through Jesus Christ is to them. However, based on the assumption that people will not receive this good news well, the countervailing commitments of wanting to maintain friendships and not being seen as a hypocrite are sufficiently potent to restrain the individual from practicing evangelism. The good news that motivates them is not as strong as the fear that they will break the other commitments by publicly sharing the good news. Second, the congregation:

Commitment That Requires Change	Doing or Not Doing to Resist Change	Worries About Other Commitments	Big Assumption Against Change
Being convinced of the good God offers in Jesus Christ for all people and the need to share it cross-culturally	Being caught up in traditional forms of evangelism focused on attracting members similar to those already in the church	Keeping the congregation healthy through strong attendance and giving; pleasing denominational or congregational leaders	If we try innovative forms of evangelism, we might drive away existing members or fail to attract new members. The church will suffer from this.

The people in this congregation recognize that God has done something good in Jesus Christ. They also believe that the good news of what God has done in Jesus can be offered across cultural and social lines. They are committed to practicing the good news in a way that will cross these boundaries, breaking out of the current practice of appealing to the same kind of people who already attend the church. However, based on the assumption that this change could drive away existing members and perhaps not successfully reach people from different contexts, the congregation chooses not to change. This at least allows the congregation to remain committed to institutional stability.

The commitments that militate against change in both examples are not intrinsically bad. It is not wrong for an individual to want to maintain good relationships with others, nor is it wrong for the congregation to desire good institutional health. The issue is not one of good versus bad commitments but of conflicting good commitments. Given this, the safest route for most individuals and organizations is to stay the course since they are already fulfilling some good commitments.

According to Kegan and Lahey, the only way to break this logic is for the individual or organization to set modest tests of the big assumptions.[4] These tests should take the form of easily attainable goals that work toward fulfilling the commitments that require change.

These goals should be easy to reach for four reasons. First, since the burden is already against change, it's unrealistic to expect that a person or organization will put more than minimal effort toward these goals. Second, the existing commitments will not be threatened by having resources diverted from them. Third, the goals will allow the person or organization seeking to change a relatively simple case to reflect on as they consider what, if any, next steps to take. Fourth, accomplishing even minor goals will start momentum toward rebalancing the commitments and practices.

This advice works for those who desire to adopt new practices of evangelism, too. By setting easily attainable goals we can move past the jam of commitments and traditionalism that forces us back to evangelism practices we have always used and that are inauthentic to our articulation of the good news. Simple goals help us avoid the notion that we are trying to transform our individual lives or local churches in one fell swoop. The small number of resources the goals require frees us to experiment with new approaches to evangelism before investing too heavily in any specific practice. And as we see the outcomes of these tests, we can generate enthusiasm for what happens when we live out our authentically held belief in the good news.

SOME PRACTICES TO CONSIDER

As with our starting points, we need to make certain our evangelistic practices are large enough. Evangelism, as we have seen, reaches into nearly every aspect of human life: spiritual, intellectual, emotional, physical, psychological, cultural, social, communal and more. It is for this reason that evangelism is often described as holistic; it invites the whole person into the good news of God. Practices of evangelism must reflect this by touching on the fullness of human life. When developing our creative practices, we should stretch our thinking to be as holistic as possible.

A well-articulated theology is helpful here. Theology, as we have seen, moves out in a spiderweb, connecting our beliefs about God, including how

---

[4]Kegan and Lahey, *Immunity to Change*, 256-72.

we believe God interacts with creation. The more deeply we have thought through our theology, the better equipped we are to consider the many ways we can share the good news of God.

What follows are several ideas that many people miss when working out their evangelistic practices. This is not because they disagree with these ideas but because they do not think about them in conjunction with evangelism. I offer them to broaden the horizon of evangelistic practice, providing more room for us to navigate in developing our authentic practices.

God as evangelist. While God has chosen to work through humans to share the good news, this does not mean God is uninvolved. Evangelism and demonstrations of God's power have long been connected to each other.

The biblical witness points to God's use of supernatural power to authenticate God's messengers. This was to give the people clear evidence of whom God had anointed to speak. In the Old Testament, this differentiation involved those who claimed to be prophets. God supported the true prophets supernaturally. In Deuteronomy 18:22, for example, God guaranteed that the predictions made by genuine prophets would be fulfilled. God also granted some prophets the ability to perform miraculous signs. Elijah's victory over the supernaturally impotent prophets of Baal on Mount Carmel demonstrated that he was the true carrier of God's message. Likewise, Elisha's miracles verified to the school of the prophets that he was chosen by God to be Elijah's successor.

God's intervention on behalf of those God has sent continues in the New Testament. Foremost, it establishes Jesus as the Messiah and as the Son of God. In Luke 7:22, Jesus lists the miracles he has performed as proof that he is the divinely sent one John the Baptist expected. In John 14:11, Jesus exhorts his disciples to believe that he is one with the Father. As evidence of this, he cites the miracles he has performed during his ministry. Christians later point to Jesus' resurrection as the chief miracle showing he was uniquely sent of God (Acts 2:32, 36).

As Jesus completes his earthly ministry, he promises that Christians will perform even greater wonders than he has as signs of the gospel's unique salvific power and their commission to preach it (Mark 16). The book of Acts picks up on this, recording numerous miracles performed by the apostles as they undertake their evangelistic work. Paul underscores the importance of these miracles in 1 Corinthians 2:4-5. He writes that the Corinthians can believe the gospel he preaches based on God's evident power in his ministry.

This same connection between evangelism and supernatural power continues over the first thousand years of the church's evangelistic efforts. Such early missionary bishops as Martin of Tours, Gregory Thaumaturgus, Porphyry of Egypt and Boniface are credited with demonstrating acts of divine power as they bring the gospel message to new populations. These miracles do more than add evidentiary weight to the gospel; they establish the superiority of the God of Jesus Christ over all other gods. As historian Ramsay MacMullen explains it, "The unique force of Christian wonder-working that does indeed need emphasis lies in the fact that it destroyed belief as well as creating it—that is, if you credited it, you then had to credit the view that went with it, denying the character of god to all other divine powers whatsoever."[5] Many stories of these wonder-working evangelists bear out MacMullen's observation, depicting the evangelists wielding the power of God to overcome pagan gods, demons and the forces of nature.

For those of us who are in parts of the church influenced by the Enlightenment, this ready acceptance of the supernatural may seem odd. We rarely hear about miracles except when people ask why there are not more of them today. This is because the Enlightenment emphasis on reason and empiricism has muffled the reports of God's miraculous activity in the church, not because God is less active today. If we are willing to break out of modernity's grip, we will see a large number of Christians ready to share experiences of the supernatural, especially in connection with evangelism.[6]

The global church gives us the opportunity to see God's work more clearly. The growth of Pentecostalism, which claims the direct intervention of the Holy Spirit in its evangelistic work, is an example of this.[7] Christians who have not had their comfort with spiritual things lessened by the Enlightenment often describe a clash of supernatural powers coinciding with their

---

[5]Ramsay MacMullen, *Christianizing the Roman Empire*: A.D. *100-400* (New Haven, CT: Yale University Press, 1984), 108-109.

[6]Craig S. Keener, a professor of New Testament, provides extensive documentation of miracles in *Miracles: The Credibility of the New Testament Accounts* (Grand Rapids: Baker, 2011).

[7]The Sentinel Group, a Pentecostal organization that makes documentaries about evangelistic revivals worldwide, has produced several resources that describe the power of the Holy Spirit breaking through what they term "spiritual oppression" as Christians dedicate themselves to God's mission, www.sentinelgroup.org.

evangelistic efforts. I have spoken with pastors from around the world who describe the need to pray against witchcraft and demons so that God will open the door for effective evangelistic outreach.

God has even bypassed human evangelists on occasion to invite people to become Christians. A fellow student in divinity school told me that she and her husband both came to the Christian faith when they independently had dreams in which Jesus and the virgin Mary appealed to them. At the time they lived in a country in which conversion to the Christian faith was illegal, yet they so strongly believed in the messages they received through their dreams that they sold everything they had and moved with their children to the United States where they could begin studying for ordained ministry. Possibly Jesus had this sort of divine action in mind when he commanded us to pray for more laborers to go into the harvest fields (Mt 9:37-38; Lk 10:2). When we cannot evangelize people directly, we can pray that God will provide other means. This might be in the form of other people but might also be through direct intervention in their lives.

Even if we step away from these dramatic descriptions of God's power, how individuals are transformed into something new when they become followers of Jesus Christ can be seen as miraculous. One of my first parishioners, who grew up in a poor town in the Appalachian Mountains of Kentucky, explained how he had seen people change when they confessed the Christian faith. He told the story of how the meanest, angriest, toughest mountain man in the area came to the altar one day to give his life to Christ. In the days, weeks and years that followed this same man became one of the gentlest and most loving people my parishioner knew. There were no grand miracles or displays of the supernatural in this story, but my parishioner firmly believed this transformation came from the power of God.

The Bible, the history of the church and the experiences of Christians throughout the world today make it plain that proclaiming the gospel message is often accompanied by acts of divine power. God is active in the evangelistic process both through equipping evangelists and by evangelizing people directly. I recognize that Christians approach the idea of God's direct intervention in a variety of ways, from the doctrine of the cessation of miracles officially espoused by Calvin, who argued that God ceased allowing miracles after the death of the apostles, to a belief that God's miraculous work is part and parcel of daily life, such as Pentecostals hold. Still, Christians have also historically understood a relationship between evangelism and God's acts of power. It is up to us to decide how to deal with this.

Winston Worrell, past president of the Academy for Evangelism in Theological Education, suggests that one way we can make room for the supernatural is by including words, deeds and signs in our evangelistic practice. Words are our articulation of what we want to share as God's good news to others. Deeds are the actions we take to embody that goodness for others. Signs are the allowance we make for God to validate the message we share through divine intervention. Worrell points to Jesus' practice of evangelism as precedent for this, demonstrating that he used all three and commissioned his disciples to do the same.[8]

It is up to each of us to navigate to our own authentic practices of evangelism, but I risk being prescriptive on this point of seeking God's direct involvement in evangelism because I firmly believe that one of the great failures of evangelism today is its reduction to a series of practices premised on human activity. If this is all evangelism is, the church is nothing but one more vendor in the marketplace of ideas trying to hawk its wares. This kind of transactional evangelism shortchanges the power of the good news. Anyone who is committed to navigating toward authentic practices of sharing the good news must learn to tack their sails to the winds of God's presence and power.

Personal formation and receiving. We often think of evangelism as a one-way practice in which the evangelist carries the good news to another person. In this scenario, the evangelist is fully equipped to share the message and the other person has nothing to do but accept or reject the evangelist's advances.

This view fails to recognize that evangelists are human and therefore subject to change, doubt and transformation. Any practice of evangelism needs to make room for the evangelist to undergo formation both in preparing to share the good news and in actually sharing it.

As we touched on briefly when we looked at the Great Commission earlier in this chapter, before Jesus sent the disciples to do their evangelistic work

---

[8]Winston Worrell (presentation, Academy for Evangelism in Theological Education, Wheaton, IL, June 21, 2013).

he gathered them to worship him and receive his instruction. Jesus did the same thing earlier in his ministry. Twice he sent out his disciples, first the twelve and later the seventy, to proclaim the coming of the kingdom. In both cases he called the disciples to him for a time of instruction first.

Jesus did not originate this practice. He followed a pattern established between God and the prophets in the Old Testament. Many of the prophets describe how God appeared to them throughout their ministries, spending time instructing and equipping them so they would be ready to share the word of God with their listeners. In Jeremiah 1 God calls Jeremiah and then initiates him into the office of prophet by teaching him to see visions and hear God's interpretation of those visions. Only after doing this does God send Jeremiah to speak to the people of Judah.

Those who would be messengers of God must put equal weight on listening and speaking. The old adage that we cannot give what we do not have is correct here. God calls the evangelist to enter into God's presence for instruction before sending the evangelist into the world. When developing our practices of evangelism we must heed this and start by considering how we will practice being in the presence of God so that God can form us as evangelists.

Our formation does not end once we are sent. Engaging with another person also carries the potential to transform us. This is true whether the other person intends it or not. Emmanuel Levinas, a French philosopher who studied encounters between people, explains this potential for transformation with the metaphor of nudity. He states that the one part of the body most people leave naked is the face. In encountering the naked face of another person, and in exposing our naked face to the other person, we experience a moment of intimacy that changes us.[9] We become bound to the other person in a way that does not allow us to exit the encounter the same as when we entered it.

Of course, we can point to numerous encounters with our fellow human beings that do not seem so transformative, such as with store clerks, delivery people and fellow passengers on airplanes or subways. We can also argue that not all cultures allow everyone to expose their face. Still, Levinas's

---

[9]Emmanuel Levinas, *Collected Philosophical Papers*, trans. Alphonso Lingis (Boston: Martinus Nijhoff Publishers, 1987), 97.

insight is helpful. The practice of evangelism should not be reduced to the impersonal level that characterizes many of our daily interactions, nor should we as evangelists partially hide from other people. We should encounter other people as equals, in a spirit of mutuality, standing ready to be transformed in the encounter.

The Bible gives us a good picture of an evangelist being formed through his encounter with those he seeks to evangelize. In Acts 18, Apollos is introduced as a fiery evangelist who moves from town to town preaching in the synagogues about Jesus Christ. When Aquila and Priscilla meet him in the synagogue at Ephesus, they recognize his potential and invite him to their home. Accepting their invitation, Apollos learns from them about the work of God through the Holy Spirit. Even though Apollos is the evangelist who comes to form others, he is open to a transformative encounter with Aquila and Priscilla. In this his faith is deepened and his ministry prospers. If Apollos had remained aloof, seeing his evangelistic work as only a matter of forming others and not of mutual relationship, his ministry might have had less of an impact.

In this example Aquila and Priscilla are already Christians. But I would argue that the same capacity to be formed by God happens in encounters with those who are not Christian. I realize that I am straying into theological assumptions here. Let me be clear about these.

My primary theological assumption is that God made humans in the image of God. That image may be tarnished, shattered and hard to recognize, but it cannot be expunged by human effort. This is true regardless of what religion, if any, the person follows or how righteous the person is. If we accept this, it provides the impetus to cultivate humility in our practice of evangelism since we are reaching out to those who bear the image of God. We never bring God to someone else but help people awaken to the connection they have with God that is theirs as a birthright of being human.

The image of God that all people share also calls us to receive God's goodness from those we evangelize. Given that all people are made in the image of God, it is possible that another person will share with us an understanding of God and the good news that we had not realized. Our practice of evangelism needs to allow us to not feel challenged when this happens. If we are enacting our beliefs authentically as we evangelize, then we can receive these new insights with joy, not fearing to show those we evangelize that we are still in the process of being formed by God.

Receiving is an underappreciated practice of evangelism. Jesus, who was the quintessential evangelist as he proclaimed the good news of the kingdom of God, is shown to receive the goodness of God from other people in all four Gospels. These include his baptism by John, his being anointed with perfume, his being worshiped and his receiving money and other necessities. In all these circumstances Jesus did not dissuade the gift givers. Rather, in his gracious receiving he encouraged those giving the gifts to continue in the divine goodness already on display in their lives. Consider what a different picture of Jesus and God we would have if Jesus had resisted these gifts rather than receiving them.

Whether spending time in the presence of God directly as we prepare to share the good news or being open to receive the goodness of God from other people while we are sharing with them, we need to make room in our practice of evangelism for the formation of the evangelist.[10] Only in doing this do we demonstrate the humility of recognizing that we do not have all the answers and that we are open to encountering God and being formed afresh in those encounters.

Scope: individual, social and ecclesiastical. It can be easy for us to reduce our evangelistic practice to activities closely associated with the theological tradition we claim. Evangelicals, Pentecostals and fundamentalists, for example, will focus on practices that invite people to personal salvation. Those following liberation theologies will emphasize advocacy on behalf of the oppressed. These sorts of practices are appropriate in light of the respective traditions. However, we should avoid limiting our practices to the most salient teachings of our traditions.

To develop our practices only by the brightest lights from our chosen traditions is to minimize the scope of our activity. This happens most frequently when we develop practices that define their outcomes only in terms of individual transformation or promoting social justice. Evangelism should encompass both of these.

---

[10]An excellent article on how evangelists can learn from those who seek to find the presence of God in their surroundings and in the people around them is Christopher B. James, "Missional Acuity: 20th Century Insights Toward a Redemptive Way of Seeing," *Witness* 26 (2012), 29-44.

Theological narrowing often comes from not understanding everything a tradition teaches. Specific traditions do favor either social or personal practices, but they rarely ignore the other completely. Liberation theology, for example, while emphasizing the need to change entire social systems, also recognizes the importance of raising individuals' awareness. People are converted from being passive participants in oppressive structures to being members of a community of justice headed by Jesus Christ. Likewise, evangelicals, Pentecostals and fundamentalists, while primarily concerned with the eternal state of a person's soul, take seriously Jesus' mandate to feed the hungry, clothe the naked and care for the sick and imprisoned. Christians in these traditions often give generously to those affected by major disasters and engage in visitation ministries at hospitals, nursing homes and prisons. It is true that liberation theology works with individuals primarily as a means for bringing social change and that evangelicalism and its related traditions often work on a social level to encourage individual salvation. Regardless, these traditions encompass both the individual and the social.

Our practices of evangelism need to be as broad in scope as the traditions that inform them, calling individuals to receive the good news of God as well as promoting God's good news in cultural and social structures. If we have trouble thinking about how our beliefs make room for practicing evangelism on these two levels, we should revisit our chosen tradition to see how it handles both.

Scope not only deals with offering the good news on individual and social levels, it also has to do with the church as a recipient of evangelism. This may sound strange. Am I suggesting that the people who make up the church are so depraved they need to hear and respond to the good news again? No. This has nothing to do with the church's faithfulness or lack thereof. Instead it has to do with the broadness of the good news we have to offer.

All people can benefit from being invited to participate more fully in the goodness of God, even those who have accepted that goodness already. Based on this, I would contend that sharing the good news should be a regular part of how people within a Christian community relate to one another.

Consider the depictions of heaven in the book of Revelation. The saints and angels are constantly bursting into song to declare the goodness of God. Only those who already live in the presence of God hear what they sing.

While the goal of these songs is not to convert anyone to believe in God, the denizens of heaven are nonetheless evangelizing each other by sharing their authentic beliefs about God with one another and inviting one another to draw more deeply into God's goodness through their praise.

In the same way, those of us within the church can practice evangelism with one another. In doing this we will accomplish two things: (1) celebrating God's goodness through Jesus Christ and (2) equipping Christians to share that goodness with those outside the church.

Evangelism is not only invitational; it is doxological. What is praise if not honoring God for God's goodness? As we share the good news with one another in the church, we also render our praise to God.

This doxological outcome of sharing the good news suggests that we can find an evangelistic prompting within every activity of a local church, regardless of whether that activity is meant for an internal or external audience. The sermon proclaims God's goodness, both praising God and calling us to live into that goodness. The sacraments acknowledge God's gracious provision for us while initiating people into (via baptism) and sustaining people in (via Communion) God's goodness. Our fellowship together provides an opportunity for us to praise God as we talk about God's goodness with one another.

We do not look for these evangelistic links so that our congregation can be seeker-sensitive or more appealing to potential new members, though we can hope that such an outcome occurs. We do it so we can bless God and each other with the goodness God has given us.

Practicing evangelism within the church also equips us to articulate and enact what we believe when we are outside the gathered Christian community. One of the greatest difficulties facing the church in North America in the early twenty-first century is that many Christians have lost the capacity to explain their core beliefs.[11] Consider what would happen if a local church explicitly used evangelism to inform its activities.

First, the people in the church would have the opportunity to practice articulating their faith. This would happen through Christian education classes and in worship where they learned the vocabulary and concepts of the faith. Second, they would experience how their belief in the good news

---

[11]Dean, *Almost Christian*, 131-56.

translated into doing good to others through service projects. Third, congregational care would show them how to live as a loving community by meeting one another's needs. Fourth, they could develop new ways of doing administration as they marshaled the church's resources and set its vision under the rubric of demonstrating the good news of God. All of these skills would translate to practices they could use to share their faith outside the church.

A question arises here: If evangelism is connected to so many ministries, how is it unique? This question assumes evangelism is a discrete practice, usually of inviting people to believe the good news. However, we are defining evangelism as a bias for the good news. This definition throws open the doors for any activity that prompts people to receive the good news to be called evangelistic.

In this sense, evangelism is more like an ethic, a core idea that informs and animates every other practice of the church. It is not something conducted by a specific committee within a local church. Those who argue that a congregation needs this or that sort of worship service, youth programming, outreach activity or fill-in-the-blank for the congregation to be more evangelistic are missing the point. Any practice that authentically embodies a congregation's celebration of God's goodness and equips the congregation to share that goodness with others is evangelistic. It doesn't matter if these activities involve a pipe organ and eighteenth-century hymns or electric guitars and the latest CCM hits. Neither is it important whether a church offers coffee and doughnut holes in the back of the sanctuary or sets up a full coffee house on the church campus. It doesn't even matter if the practices are carried out in a megachurch with a massive staff and ample resources or in a tiny church with a small group of volunteers doing the best they can with what they have. If the activities are authentic means of celebrating God's goodness and equipping people to share that goodness, then evangelism is being practiced.

Likewise, questions about whether "evangelistic" activities are somehow going to water down the true purpose of the church are also misplaced. Nothing about the work of the church should fail to celebrate God's goodness or equip God's people to share God's goodness. Any ministry of the church that is not evangelistic in this sense is not what it should be anyway.

To be clear, I am not advocating against congregations dedicating re-sources toward welcoming visitors and inviting people to accept the Christian faith. I am stating that these activities should not be confused with the fullness of evangelism. Evangelism should just as actively invite those inside the church to know and share in God's goodness as it invites those outside the church to do the same. We fall into reductionism when we think we no longer need to be evangelized because we have crossed the threshold into the church community.

The area in which we navigate evangelism is a large one. It includes how we share the good news for the transformation of individuals, cultures and social structures outside the church, how we praise God and how we edify one another within the church. Given the cosmic scope of God's goodness, this makes sense. We should plan on making several stops along our route as we navigate evangelism, welcoming onboard as many activities and min-istries as we can in our journey to an authentic practice of evangelism.

Individual and corporate evangelism. This wide scope of action requires us to practice evangelism as individuals and as a community. But it can be difficult to keep in mind that we are both individual evangelists and par-ticipants in a larger evangelistic community. The modern and postmodern press for individualism encourages us to develop practices we think we can accomplish alone. At the same time, the institutional need for growth makes us think of large, specific practices for an entire congregation. We would do better to think of our individual practice as contributing to the larger practice of an entire community. We are not a lone ship navigating evan-gelism but part of an armada. While each of us may chart our course somewhat differently, we maneuver within the same Christian Tradition propelled forward by the same good news. This means we can coordinate our individual practices so we have a larger, more holistic practice provided by the community of faith.

Understanding ourselves as part of a large web of evangelists reminds us that the outcome of evangelism does not fall entirely on the individual. A major reason Christians are uncomfortable with evangelism is the heavy weight they feel it places on them as individuals. It is unnerving to think God expects us to obey the various evangelistic commands in the Bible as indi-viduals (Ezekiel 33 is especially intimidating!). We hear the requirements to call nations back from unjust practices, to teach people to live according to the ways of Jesus and to reach everyone around the world. It is too much! Yet many Christians believe this is exactly the burden God has called us to bear.

If we shift our way of thinking about evangelism so that it is not an activity required of individuals only but is carried out by many Christians together, it is not so overwhelming. Each of us is called to fulfill our part in the practice, but no one of us is responsible for it all.

Consider how this might work in the case of sharing the good news with a specific individual. An individual Christian might meet and have conversations with this individual. This one Christian can share her or his faith with the individual and demonstrate what it means to live that faith in daily life. This is good as far as it goes, but it is even better if the Christian can invite the individual to see a community of Christians living that faith. The Christians in the community can demonstrate God's goodness in how they relate to each other, giving the evangelized person an opportunity to see what lives grounded in the good news look like. More than that, the community can welcome the individual to explore what it's like to be part of the community. This can happen even before the person makes a decision to accept the good news, allowing him or her to "belong before believing."[12] The strength of this corporate relationship with the individual makes the evangelism more effective than what the single Christian could have done alone.

The corporate practices of evangelism do not make individual practices less important. Human relationships still occur one on one. Before there is an opportunity to draw people into a community there is usually a connection between two individuals. However, the community takes the pressure off the individual evangelist because all the people in the community share the work of evangelism.

The individual and corporate practices of evangelism are one seamless whole. The two interlock as people from within the community meet and build relationships with people outside the community. Individual Christians become bridges connecting those outside with the community. The community as a whole takes on the role of demonstrating the good news in practice and forming those who desire to claim this good news for themselves.

---

[12]Robin Gill, *A Vision for Growth: Why Your Church Doesn't Have to Be a Pelican in the Wilderness* (London: SPCK, 1994), 27-28.

Immersive storytelling. Since the good news we share is better conveyed as a narrative than a set of propositions, we should consider how to practice evangelism as an immersive act of storytelling. The more creatively and winsomely we do this, the more we help people recognize how they can weave their lives into the vast goodness God offers through Jesus Christ.

The church offers a deep set of resources for this immersive work, including its liturgy, calendar, architecture and rituals. The divine liturgy in the Eastern Orthodox tradition is an excellent example of how all these resources can be used to draw people into the good news. The liturgy tells the story of how God has come into the world as Jesus Christ, opening the door for people to enter the divine life of God. This weekly narrative is deepened by the church calendar, with each season emphasizing a different aspect of the story. Special rituals punctuate the calendar year to highlight important parts of the story. Throughout, the architecture of the church, including its icons, candles and incense, prompt worshipers to recognize that this story is not of the world but comes from and carries them back to the kingdom of God.

The evangelistic power of the divine liturgy is seen in a famous story concerning the conversion of Russia. Prince Vladimir of Kiev sent envoys to determine which religion was most proper to follow. The envoys traveled extensively and attended the worship services of several religions but remained unimpressed. Finally, they arrived at Hagia Sophia in Constantinople. Their report to the prince demonstrated the immersive power of the church: "We knew not whether we were in heaven or on earth. We cannot describe it to you; we only know that God dwells there among human beings, and their service surpasses the worship of all other places. For we cannot forget that beauty."[13]

In most Protestant churches it is easy to overlook the immersive power of liturgy, calendar, architecture and rituals when practicing evangelism. The mantra since the 1990s has been to welcome new people by confronting them with as few alien symbols and practices as possible. This led many churches to take down altars, crosses and other identifiably Christian images that might be uncomfortable for newcomers to face.

---

[13]*The Russian Primary Chronicle*, Laurentian text (Cambridge, MA: Medieval Academy of America, 1953), 110-11.

It is important for us to be welcoming, but in conceding the physical space and practices of the church we also minimize our commitment to sharing the good news. Since evangelism not only introduces people to the good news but forms them in it, we should not be quick to jettison those aspects of church life that were developed to aid that formation. Many Christian missionaries made it one of their priorities to establish identifiably Christian spaces and practices early in their evangelistic efforts. They did this to make use of their formative power among those they sought to reach.[14]

A middle ground between the desire not to overcome those new to the church with the unknown and the desire to immerse them in the story of God's goodness through Jesus Christ is possible. This takes place when the church uses its unique space and practices but has interpreters available. These interpreters can help new people get their bearings and enter more fully into the story. Equipping these interpreters may require the church to explain its storytelling apparatus to its own members, many of whom also may not realize how immersive the church's practices are! One way I used to do this in my congregations was to take the children on a short field trip of the sanctuary about once a quarter. I did this during the worship service and explained to the children what we saw. This drew both them and the adults into the story and equipped them to interpret the symbols and practices of the church to those who were new in our midst.

This immersive storytelling does not need to reside in the church only. Art, whether painting, sculpture, filmmaking, music or any other sort of artistic expression, is a powerful means for inviting people to immerse themselves in the story of God's goodness. This art can and should be exhibited in mainstream cultural venues. Creative Paradox, an organization in Annapolis, Maryland, with a mission of "cultivating a vibrant network of artists who glorify God and impact culture" (see creativeparadox.org), is an excellent example of this.

By using these means of immersive storytelling we can bypass people's guardedness about evangelism. Individuals can be drawn into the movie, the picture, the flow of the liturgy, the music or whatever method we use to

---

[14]One recent example of this was the home missionary work done to evangelize settlers in the American Wild West. See Mark R. Teasdale, "Reclaiming Montanans: The Evangelistic Endeavours of Brother Van," *Wesley and Methodist Studies* 4 (2012): 129-40.

share the story and encounter God's goodness. We invite them to work out the meaning and power of what God has done through Jesus Christ for themselves. If we tell the story well enough, they will choose to stay immersed and begin to draw the connections between the metanarrative of the good news and their own life stories.

HOSPITALITY, RECONCILIATION, STEWARDSHIP

I end this chapter with three Christian practices that are often overlooked in relation to evangelism: hospitality, reconciliation and stewardship. Hospitality is the practice of entering a mutual relationship with another person in which each has the opportunity to care for and be cared for by the other. Reconciliation is the practice of healing relationships. Stewardship is the practice of making use of what God gives us. Each of these practices has entire sets of books dedicated to it, so this brief section is not meant to offer a full overview of any of them. It is simply meant to show some of the salient connections between them and the practice of evangelism.

Hospitality is often thought of as offering something nice to a guest, such as inviting the neighbors over for a cookout, serving dinner and providing beds for the homeless in the local church, or even offering refreshments after a worship service. But these common understandings of hospitality fall short of the full Christian practice of hospitality. Christian hospitality is a practice of creating mutuality between the host and guest.[15]

Mutuality is established when both people in the relationship are recognized as having authority. The host initiates this by paying attention to the other person so as to be aware of what he or she needs. By paying attention rather than acting unilaterally, the host grants authority to the guest to decide what need the host will meet. The host then exercises authority by meeting the need.

Christian hospitality goes beyond this. It is not content with the roles of host and guest remaining static, as if only one person had needs and the other an inexhaustible set of resources. In Christian hospitality the host also pays attention to gifts the guest can offer and how those gifts might meet the

---

[15]Christine D. Pohl, *Making Room: Recovering Hospitality as a Christian Tradition* (Grand Rapids: Eerdmans: 1999), 72; and Amy Oden, *And You Welcomed Me: A Sourcebook on Hospitality in Early Christianity* (Nashville: Abingdon, 2001), 26-27.

host's need. This is not a matter of payment or a demand for gratitude. It is creating the opportunity for mutuality. Both become hosts; both become guests. Both are made whole by the presence and support of the other. The most prominent biblical example of this is Jesus Christ in the town of Emmaus after the resurrection. He comes into the house as a guest invited to dinner. In breaking the bread, he becomes the giver of life to his hosts.

This mutual meeting of needs has clear implications for the practice of evangelism. Richard Peace has described evangelism as "offering people hospitality to explore spiritual things."[16] Christians should start not by offering the good news but by paying attention to the needs of the people to whom we would offer it. In doing this we grant them the authority to determine how we share the good news with them.

Once we know how to share with them, we share the best we have. This means offering the good news with excellence and authenticity while remaining willing to hear and see what they have to offer us. We are not the only ones with answers. We are a welcoming host who has good things to offer and who is ready to receive good things from our guests, too.

Hospitality and evangelism are related in another way as well. Often an uneasy relationship exists between the church's role as evangelist and its role as a provider of physical or monetary aid to people in need. We want to share our gifts with others freely, but we also want people to know we are helping them because we are Christians and not just another social agency. Churches tend to balance this by offering aid based on our own agendas. We give what is easiest to give when it is easiest to give it, setting up a variety of requirements for how people can receive from us. We reject anything else as unreasonable. Additionally, we give as efficiently as possible, leaving little time for us to connect with the people we are helping, much less pay attention long enough to build mutuality with them.

Both evangelism and hospitality argue that this sort of practice falls short of embodying the good news of God for others. While it is critical to create practices that account for what and how we distribute to those in need, we must develop those practices so that we interact with those in need with mutuality. They should not position us perpetually as the wealthy hosts and

---

[16]Richard Peace (presentation, Academy for Evangelism in Theological Education, Northbrook, IL, June 16, 2011).

them perpetually as the needy guests. Moreover, the interaction should leave room for relationship building so that those in need are welcome to become fellow participants in our communities of faith.

Reconciliation has grown in importance as a Christian practice over the twentieth century as racial, ethnic, national and international conflicts have burst forth. These huge divisions add to the broken relationships many people experience in their daily lives. Reconciliation is essential because it promises that all can be healed and peace be restored. If we want our vision of the good news to have meaning for much of the world today, we need to provide this healing.

Missiologist Robert Schreiter explains that evangelism and reconciliation have multiple points in common. These are visible in the four practices he details as essential to reconciliation: (1) healing the individuals or parties that have been hurt in the conflict, (2) telling the truth about what has happened so that the harm can be recognized and overcome, (3) working for justice by overcoming inequalities or structural issues that make one group less capable of sharing in the reconciliation than the other and (4) encouraging each side to forgive the other.[17] That these practices fit within the call for Christians to demonstrate a bias for the good news is clear. Our specific traditions will shape how we move through this process of reconciliation, but there is no doubt that by being agents of reconciliation we are also practitioners of evangelism.

Schreiter also recognizes that reconciliation is necessary not only among people but between people and God. He points to 2 Corinthians 5:18-20 in which St. Paul describes his evangelistic work as imploring people to be reconciled to God through Jesus Christ. Again, our traditions will explain differently how God makes reconciliation possible through Jesus. Notwithstanding, this creates another link between reconciliation and evangelism, with the proclamation of the good news of God serving as a means of reconciling people to the goodness God desires for them.

Far from the crass fundraising we often associate with it, stewardship is the care of all things God has given to us. Stewardship understands that all we have—our money, our possessions, our health, our mental abilities, our

---

[17]Robert Schreiter, "The Message of Reconciliation as an Effective Vehicle for Evangelization," *Witness: The Journal of the Academy for Evangelism in Theological Education* 29 (2014): 16-19.

ability to participate in culture and social structures, and everything else—belongs to God. God gives us use of these things for a period of time and will call us to account for how we have used them. Jesus describes this in several parables that deal with the relationships between master and steward.

How we use our resources offers a window into what we value and what we believe God values. This is the point at which stewardship and evangelism connect. If we are biased for the good news, believing that God desires all people to enter into God's goodness through Jesus Christ, then the way we spend our money, our time and our energy should show that. This is true for individual Christians and for congregations.

Douglas John Hall goes so far as to declare that stewardship can be understood as the vocation God has given to humanity.[18] If we are faithful in this mission by using our resources as God would have us use them, we will please God. We will also give people watching us a reason to ask why we use our resources the way we do. Hall has a brilliant conclusion in which he makes this case:

> "Why, Christian, do you strive for the welfare of this second-rate planet? Why do you seek justice for these wretched oppressed people on the margins of the great world? Why do you give up your shares in profitable multinationals—why all this divesting? Why do you struggle against inequality, starvation, and despair? Why are you expending so much psychic energy in the pursuit of peace? What is peace? Why have you identified yourself with these disappearing species? . . . Why are you still trying to make hope work?" And then—but mostly only then—the Christians would tell their story, judiciously, and unpretentiously. Then they would give the reason for their hope. . . . And would it not be authentic mission, being the response to a question and not, as so much of what has called itself mission has been, answers to questions nobody asked. Being grounded in participation, in solidarity with the general and earthly condition and not just another petty ideology vying for the souls of human beings.[19]

Stewardship reminds us that each purchase, each minute passed and each exertion toward accomplishing something is a testimony to whether we are investing ourselves in the goodness of God. Hall adds that the world is

---

[18]Douglas John Hall, *The Steward: A Biblical Symbol Come of Age* (Grand Rapids: Eerdmans, 1991), 122.
[19]Ibid., 257-58.

watching this testimony and will render its decision on the good news we proclaim based on what it sees.

I hope it is clear by now that I am not arguing for the adoption of specific practices of evangelism but providing insights that help us navigate the

LEARNING ACTIVITY

Field trips to ministries that specialize in the practices of hospitality, reconciliation and stewardship can give us concrete examples of the evangelistic nature of these practices. For example, I have taken my students to a coffee house run by a pastor whose primary form of ministry is hospitality. Set in a highly intellectual population where Christianity is not well received, his space is designed to make people feel comfortable discussing spiritual things. He hopes that in time they will be ready to learn about Jesus from other Christians. In the meantime he provides hospitality that includes glimpses of the goodness of God in how he treats them.

I have taken my students to a Catholic food pantry distribution site where workers overcome the provider-recipient dichotomy. They do this by setting up the site as a grocery store and assigning a personal shopper to walk with the clients as they push their carts through the aisles. All the food is free, but the structure gives the clients a sense of agency, as if they were shopping in a regular store. The personal shopper also has a chance to hold a conversation with the client and learn about her or him, providing the potential for a relationship to develop. All of this maintains the dignity of the client.

We have also visited a prayer-walking ministry. This ministry looks for parts of the city that have experienced crime or other difficulties during the past week. Its members go on Saturday mornings to anoint those places with oil and pray over them. They pray for reconciliation among the people of the city and for reconciliation between the people of the city and God.

Finally, a colleague of mine takes students to a variety of local farming cooperatives and other faith-based environmental initiatives. These demonstrate an excellent picture of stewardship of the earth.

often tricky route of putting our evangelism into practice. Those practices should reflect our authentic beliefs, which we have articulated in our respective starting points and further defined through our theological reflection. They should be holistic, recognizing that those being evangelized are multifaceted and need to have evangelism demonstrate God's goodness to them on multiple levels, including individually, culturally and socially. They also should be creative, making room for God, individuals and communities of Christians to serve as evangelists.

The more we generate wide-ranging, creative practices that are authentic to what we believe about the good news, the closer we come to our destination. We have navigated through the process of interrogating, articulating and theologically reflecting on our beliefs. We have made our way through the contextual gauntlet, and we have maneuvered through difficulties in making our beliefs concrete in our practices. All that is left is to look at the larger implications of our successful navigation.

Chapter Six

Evangelizing Yourself,
Evangelizing the World

*O*ne Christmas my wife and I had the opportunity to visit Belgrade, Serbia. This was in the 1990s prior to the NATO bombing and when the socialist government was beginning to loosen its controls on the people.

A result of the government's less stringent oversight was a sudden upsurge of people attending church. Reclaiming their centuries-old Christian heritage, Serbs swarmed back to the Serbian Orthodox Church, especially on major holidays. This Christmas was no exception.

On Christmas Eve my wife and I decided to attend the service being presided over by the patriarch of the Serbian Orthodox Church. It was being held in the Cathedral of St. Michael the Archangel, which is directly across the street from the patriarch's residence and offices. We made our way through the crowds of people who likewise hoped to worship with the patriarch, and we found a place in the church.

The cathedral was gorgeous. Rather than the traditional onion-dome Byzantine style that marks most Eastern Orthodox church architecture, it was constructed in a baroque style. It displayed enormous frescoes on the ceiling depicting various scenes from the life of Jesus Christ.

A young Serbian boy standing near us was craning his neck to look at the pictures of Christ. My wife, who is fluent in Serbian, asked him if he knew the stories behind the pictures. He replied that he did not. She told me this, and I offered to tell the stories of the pictures while my wife translated. The boy readily accepted, and I began a simple narration of the paintings soaring over us.

As I spoke and my wife translated, we noticed that the crowd, which was already shoulder to shoulder in the standing-room-only space, began to draw closer around us. It became evident that many people beyond the boy were curious about the stories of Christ.

The Serbs have been Christians since the ninth century, and the particular church we were in had been standing for over 150 years when we visited it. Yet with all this surrounding them to teach them of the good news of God through Jesus Christ in the power of the Holy Spirit, most Serbs remained ignorant of that news.

Navigating our way through evangelism forces us to be intentional about articulating what we believe and developing practices that authentically embody those beliefs. If we do not move through this entire process, we end up with a wealth of Christian wisdom on our hands and no capacity to use it. We are neither formed by it nor are we able to invite others to share it.

The need to clarify what we believe and why we believe it, to be contextually sensitive and to creatively practice our faith is greater now than it has been for over a century. This is especially true in the West where there has been a steady decline not only in the number of people who identify themselves as Christians but in cultural respect for the benefits Christianity has provided.

The erosion of Christian influence is most visible in something that Christians from all theological traditions can recognize: the slow and steady failing of human rights. Catholic scholars Mike Aquilina and Jim Papandrea explain that the Christian faith brought with it "cultural revolutions that gave the world a concern for human rights in two general categories: the protection of all human life, and the protection of each person's dignity."[1] With the loss of the Christian metanarrative in the West, however, these revolutions are being undone. Os Guinness describes this as the West severing its religious roots. He states, "If the original Jewish and Christian foundations of human dignity, liberty and equality are to be rejected, the ideas themselves need to be transposed to a new key or eventually they will wither. The Western world now stands as a cut-flower civilization, and such once-vital convictions have a seriously shortened life."[2]

---

[1]Mike Aquilina and James L. Papandrea, *Seven Revolutions: How Christianity Changed the World and Can Change It Again* (New York: Image, 2015), 6.
[2]Os Guinness, *The Global Public Square: Religious Freedom and the Making of a World Safe for*

If the erosion of human rights results from a loss of Christian values in the culture, then an important part of regaining those rights is evangelism. This is not only because evangelism invites people into the Christian good news that serves as the bedrock for human rights but because evangelism depends on a culture and social structures that protect people's ability to practice their faith. It also depends on people having the freedom to follow their conscience by accepting new beliefs. It is not too much to say that engaging in evangelism is a quintessential act of exercising and supporting human rights.

Evangelism does more than replant Western human rights in its native soil of the Christian faith. It also wards off the increasing danger of seductive and dangerous ideologies seeking to claim converts. In the mid-2010s the news is rife with reports of radicalization as people leave comfortable lives in the West to join the ranks of the Islamic State and other terrorist groups. They do it because they have found something deeper in these groups' teachings, as disturbing as they are, than the weak claims of secularization. Governments have set up a variety of counter-radicalization efforts, but these have been only marginally successful. This problem is not a matter of policy; it is a battle for people's souls. As Guinness puts it, officials are "tone deaf" to this reality.[3] Only by meeting these radical claims with evangelism will we be able to

---

LEARNING ACTIVITY

As a final step in navigating evangelism, we should give the outcome of our work a title. Giving something a title demands that we distill its essence into a few words. Ending the process with developing a title brings our articulation of what we believe to its fullest expression.

There are several examples of possible titles. Some include evangelism as initiation into the kingdom of God, evangelism as virtuous witness and evangelism as extravagant welcoming. There is no wrong title. Whatever your title is will help you highlight what you think is most important about evangelism.

Diversity (Downers Grove, IL: InterVarsity Press, 2013), 67.
[3]Ibid., 135.

overcome the immersive radicalization narrative. As we do this we can invite people to move from the demonstrably bad news of radicalization to the deeper and life-affirming good news of Jesus Christ.

Evangelism has long been connected to the Christian idea of salvation. To engage in it is more than to work for the salvation of individual souls. Evangelism is an act by which we seek to save the world.

SAVING OURSELVES

To work toward this grand conclusion of evangelism, we must commit ourselves to navigating through our beliefs and practices. As we do this we will find several benefits in addition to the salvific outcomes of evangelism.

Claiming the mantle of evangelist. One of the most unexpected benefits is salvaging how we view ourselves and our congregations in reference to evangelism. Where we once may have thought we were incapable of evangelism, we can become comfortable with seeing ourselves as evangelists. Several of my students have experienced this.

One student was a stay-at-home mom who was convinced she had nothing to do with evangelism because she rarely moved outside of her domestic sphere. After navigating through her beliefs, though, she realized the way she loved her children and taught them to love one another was an act of evangelism. It embodied her understanding of the love of God and spread that love.

Another student told me she nearly turned down ordination because she consistently scored poorly in the "evangelism" category of a spiritual inventory her denomination had her take. The authors of these tools often define evangelism narrowly, based on revivalism stereotypes. By navigating through her beliefs and recognizing the ways she could creatively share the good news of God, she was able to refute these results. She shifted from seeing evangelism as a weakness to seeing it as a strength, and she has maintained it as a hallmark of her ministry ever since.

Another student was the pastor of a small rural church. He was depressed because his church had not grown for several years. That the town in which he served was decreasing in population and that his church building was difficult to find were beside the point for him. Year after year he saw the negative trend in the annual statistics and felt like a failure. After reflecting on what his congregation believed about God's goodness and how it embodied that belief, though, he came to a new conclusion. As farmers who understood what it meant to receive aid from neighbors when they faced natural disasters, the members of his church wanted to show God's goodness by embodying that aid for others. Accordingly, for many years his congregation packed more supplies to send to people affected by floods, hurricanes, tornadoes and other disasters than all the churches of his denomination in the same county put together. Before, he had dismissed this as simple do-goodism that did not count for much. He came to recognize that this was an authentic practice of sharing the good news.

Catechesis in local churches and seminaries. An additional benefit of navigating evangelism is that it can provide an entryway to catechesis for new and existing Christians. Rather than leaving evangelism in the far back of what we discuss, we can invite those within a church community to articulate what holds them most firmly to the Christian faith. As we do this, we can connect their ideas with the doctrines and theological traditions of the community they have joined. This will give people in the church the opportunity to express their authentic beliefs and have those beliefs formed simultaneously.

A seminary can use evangelism in a similar way. It can encourage its students to navigate through their own beliefs and practices even as it teaches them the technical language of the theological disciplines. This will provide students with experiential hooks to attach to their lessons. Evangelism also offers the students a way to interrogate the academic fields they encounter, allowing them to organize what they learn around the central axis of the good news. See the appendix for a detailed discussion of how the study of evangelism interrelates with theological education more broadly. Also, see the online teaching material for sample syllabi and conversations on how to teach evangelism.

LEARNING ACTIVITY

It is helpful to meet one on one with others when we first try putting our beliefs in words. This gives us a chance to practice articulating our beliefs verbally and to receive feedback at a time when it is still relatively easy for us to rethink and revise how we explain what we believe.

Sparking meaningful conversation for church leaders. A third benefit to the process of navigating evangelism is that it can be done corporately. A congregation or a church leadership team can initiate conversation about the group's core beliefs and how the ministries and programs under its purview are or are not demonstrating those beliefs. This can be done either as a stand-alone activity or in conjunction with a visioning retreat or similar event. One congregation I worked with used this process to help them discern whether to undertake a major capital campaign. The leaders wanted to be certain they kept their bias for the good news and their desire to share that good news foremost so that the facilities they were contemplating served this mission. They knew that expensive facilities quickly become a congregation's mission if there is no articulated mission for the facilities to serve.

To use this material in a local context, see the online teaching materials. They include a sample agenda for navigating evangelism as part of a leadership retreat and a modified version of a SWOT (strengths, weaknesses, opportunities, threats) analysis. This is a useful tool for church leaders to use to determine how their core beliefs in the good news match with their congregation's actual ministry practices.

Discovering new role models. A fourth benefit of navigating evangelism is that we can begin to appreciate new role models for the practice of evangelism. Traditionally we have allowed people to self-identify as evangelists. This is one of the reasons evangelists have had such a bad name; there was no standard to meet for someone to claim the title of evangelist. However, when we expand our thinking so that evangelism includes any activity that embodies the good news of God, we can identify new people as exemplars of evangelism.

> ### LEARNING ACTIVITY
>
> We can benefit from learning about practices of leadership alongside evangelism. I have seen this when I team-teach a seminary course with a professor of leadership and we discuss the intersection of evangelism and leadership in a congregational context. This is especially important for those who are called to plant or revitalize churches. These jobs require us to be excellent evangelists and excellent administrators.

These new role models may not overtly move people to follow Jesus Christ, but they do an exceptional job of helping people recognize the goodness of God. It is not that Jesus is unimportant to these people, but the role they play in the church's corporate work of evangelism does not entail introducing people to him. This meshes with Richard Peace's idea of evangelism as hospitality and Andy Crouch's idea of culture creation. The Christian who embodies the good news of God creates a situation in which people can live into that goodness. As they do this, God can draw them to Jesus Christ through other evangelists in the Christian community. The fact that an individual evangelist does not preside over the entire process of someone explicitly acknowledging God's work through Jesus Christ does not negate that person's role as an evangelist.

I have come to see the late Fred Rogers, host of the children's show *Mr. Rogers' Neighborhood*, as one of the greatest evangelists of the twentieth century. A Presbyterian minister, he never mentioned God during his program. But his presentations were remarkable means of inviting people into God's goodness. His gentle and fun-loving demeanor immediately put people at ease, opening them to his words of instruction. There was nothing coercive in his approach. Rather, his consistent message was that people should see beauty in the world, especially in each other, and should eschew anything harmful to themselves and others. Along with this instruction he unfailingly reminded his viewers that they had deep intrinsic worth regardless of the labels others placed on them. He was careful to include a diversity of people, including people of different races, with different jobs, with disabilities and from different countries, as guests on his show. He also deployed a variety of creative practices, including puppets, songs and field trips to other locations in his "neighborhood," as means of showing how robust his message was and how immersive it could be.

I certainly don't expect everyone to see Mr. Rogers as the archetypal evangelist. But I do hope we can see him as wonderful example of a new role model in navigating evangelism. I am grateful that Mr. Rogers can help guide me to share the good news of what God has done for us through Jesus Christ alongside people like St. Paul, Thérèse of Lisieux and Billy Graham.

Farewell to guilt. A final benefit is that navigating evangelism can release us from the guilt that so often attends evangelism. It releases us from the individual guilt we feel for not carrying the full work of evangelism ourselves by reminding us that evangelism is the work of God through the whole people of God. No one individual is called to shoulder the entire process of meeting, sharing, inviting and forming another person in the Christian faith. As communities of faith we are released from the guilt of not measuring up to marketplace-driven expectations focused on our congregation's numbers. It is not that we are unaware of our numbers or do not care if we grow; it is that we are free to develop metrics that measure whether we are sharing the goodness of God in ways that are authentic to us. If we can demonstrate that we are bearing fruit by these practices, we can rightly claim to be effective evangelistically regardless of what the numbers say.

What becomes clear in these benefits is that navigating evangelism liberates us from the negativism, judgmentalism and discouragement that have too often found homes in our churches. This is both ironic and satisfying, since these are the very terms that many people would apply to evangelism. To navigate evangelism well is not only to break out of this stereotype but to become a force God uses to break these curses for others.

To navigate evangelism well is to navigate our way to an authentic faith as we claim what we have experienced to be the good news of God through Jesus Christ in the power of the Holy Spirit.

To navigate evangelism well is to navigate theology well as we reflect on and articulate what we believe and why we believe it.

To navigate evangelism well is to navigate relationships within the church well as we learn to practice reconciliation by seeing the good that Christians from all theological traditions have to offer and linking arms with them to support each other in sharing that good.

To navigate evangelism well is to navigate context well as we develop communities of faith that will cultivate space for Christians to create new forms of culture that can transform the larger culture and society.

To navigate evangelism well is to navigate the vast scope of Christian practice well, finding creative ways to embody the good news that are authentic to what we believe.

To navigate evangelism well is to navigate theological education well, giving us a lens that lets us see the connections among the fields we study as well as the connection between the work of the academy and our practices of faith.

To navigate evangelism well is to navigate our world well, working to save it from the forces that would destroy it and instilling in it the good news that will bring it life.

What I Wish
I Knew When I
Started Seminary

I remember my first day—really my first minute—of seminary vividly. As class started, the professor lifted the Bible and said, "Most professors would throw this on the floor to show that it is just a book. I will not do that, but I will tell you that I think most of it is fiction." I don't remember a thing after that. I was too shocked. This was not an auspicious start for a kid who had gone to a youth group that taught about the inerrancy of the Scriptures! And, as I saw it, things only got worse for me over the next two years.

I was confronted by entirely different ideas about what the Christian faith meant. I knew what I believed, but I often felt like my beliefs were scattered. I had a loose confederation of beliefs, not a coherent faith that could transfer across all the required courses I had to take.

It wasn't until I met the evangelism professor that I felt like I could start putting together the pieces of my beliefs. With his aid in the classroom and during numerous visits to his office, I began to find my way in seminary. He helped me articulate God's good news. With this in place, I had a framework for understanding and responding to what I encountered as I moved from class to class and was introduced to new academic fields. I became so comfortable in the seminary that I ended up never leaving it!

What I wish I'd known at the beginning of my studies, when I was staring in horror at my first seminary professor, was how evangelism could help me in my theological education. This appendix is my attempt at offering the insight I gained after the fact.

At the beginning of any journey we must spend time preparing for what we may face ahead. Only with the proper maps, gear and directions are we ready to navigate to our destination. Evangelism is no different. To do it well, we need to equip ourselves with the critical tools and insights that theological education has to offer if we are to reflect on, articulate and practice the good news.

However, theological education itself requires some navigation. This is where the study of evangelism can help. Evangelism not only benefits from the lessons of other theological fields but also provides us a way to approach them. It can do this because evangelism is not a field of study in its own right. A field of study has its own unique content and set of academic methodologies for analyzing that content. Evangelism is not like this. Both its content and methodologies are drawn from a variety of fields. This makes it, as the late James C. Logan used to describe it, a "nexus point" of academic fields. William Abraham agrees with this, arguing that evangelism is a "field-encompassing field," meaning that the study of evangelism requires interaction with a variety of academic disciplines.[1]

Evangelism is also a practical theology, meaning that it integrates academic theology with everyday life. It takes the notion of praxis seriously by recognizing that how people think influences how they act, and how they act shapes what they think. As with all practical theologies, evangelism is messy because it tries to make sense out of what people do, and people are rarely ordered in their activities.

Placing evangelism at the center of our theological education provides order to this messiness. It puts the tools of the various disciplines we study at our disposal to help us navigate evangelism with greater clarity and skill. At the same time, an insistence on making the good news the heart of the Christian faith provides us with a touchstone from which we can interrogate and organize the different disciplines we are studying.

Consider Linus from the *Peanuts* comic. Linus is engaged in an evangelistic activity when he shares the good news of the Great Pumpkin with others. This evangelism by Linus leads to a complex set of questions that require the tools of several academic fields to answer.

---

[1] William J. Abraham, "Teaching Evangelism," *Journal of the Academy for Evangelism in Theological Education* 17 (2001-2002): 7.

First, there is the message that Linus proclaims about the Great Pumpkin. What authority does he draw on to ground this story? Does he appeal to some sort of holy writ? If so, is his hermeneutic of sincerity—the most important trait for appeasing the Great Pumpkin—a sound one? These are questions that, in theological education, would be explored in biblical studies classes with their analysis both of the biblical text and the ways people read that text.

Second, consider the way Linus has organized his belief system regarding the Great Pumpkin. There is the doctrine of the existence and nature of the Great Pumpkin (he exists and is benevolent to those who wait for him in sincerity). There is the incarnation of the Great Pumpkin (he is manifest in a bodily form). There is a soteriology (the Great Pumpkin judges the sincerity of those who wait for him and justifies the sincerest by appearing in their pumpkin patch and giving them gifts). Questions arise, though. Are these appropriate categories for Linus to use to organize his thinking about the Great Pumpkin? Are they true to his authority? Are they skewed, knowingly or unknowingly, by Linus being a white, middle-class male who lives in the suburban United States? In the world of Christian theological education, these questions would be the domain of systematic theology as it plumbs what we believe and why we organize our beliefs as we do.

Closely related to this, we must ask whether Linus has any historical tradition behind his devotion to the Great Pumpkin. Are there groups of people who have organized their beliefs about the Great Pumpkin in a similar way as Linus? Are there exemplars of sincerity that Linus can look to for direction or inspiration in living out his beliefs in the Great Pumpkin? Have the tides of culture and time caused changes, schisms, mergers or other events that have shaped beliefs or practices associated with the Great Pumpkin? These are all questions that would be answered by the field of history.

How does Linus's belief in the Great Pumpkin form him as a person? At the minimum it shapes his decisions about how to spend Halloween night. Rather than enjoying the sure gratification of trick-or-treating and attending the Halloween party, he sits in a pumpkin patch he has cultivated to demonstrate his sincere belief that the Great Pumpkin will come. The fact that he has cultivated the pumpkins shows that his beliefs stretch beyond

Halloween night. Pumpkins take several months to grow, so he has intentionally set aside the resources necessary to raise this crop throughout the summer and early fall. Are there other ways his beliefs form him? Do they cause Linus to modify how he relates to other people? Does he consider how the Great Pumpkin will judge other decisions and activities beyond the sincerity of the actual pumpkin patch? These questions belong to theological ethics, which studies how theological beliefs form people.

How does Linus translate his beliefs into practice? He writes letters to the Great Pumpkin, enduring the scorn of local children and dogs alike. He adopts the ascetic ritual of waiting in the cold pumpkin patch on Halloween night. He invites Sally and others to sit with him in anticipation of the Great Pumpkin arising. When Sally joins him, he catechizes her in the basic beliefs of the Great Pumpkin. He is wary of the language he uses (he must say "when the Great Pumpkin comes," not "if the Great Pumpkin comes"). All these practices are under the purview of the various forms of practical theology, which analyze how we practice our beliefs. Spiritual formation considers the disciplines we use to communicate with God, homiletics how we proclaim our faith, worship how we ritually enact our adoration of God, and Christian education how we impart our beliefs to others.

What is the context in which he practices his beliefs? What are the prevailing cultural values and rituals? We see some of this by how the other children in *Peanuts* act on Halloween night. We also see what happens when one of those children decides to give up her participation in the culturally acceptable practices to join Linus. These contextual issues can be approached through studies addressing cultural analysis.

All this from a cartoon in which a child tries to convince his friends that an enormous, sentient squash-man will give sincere people presents on a special day each year! This is the power of holding evangelism at the heart of our theological educational endeavors. As we navigate through the sometimes choppy waters of evangelism, we also chart a course that helps us learn the other subjects in our curriculum, integrate the ideas from those subjects and stay connected to how people live outside of the classroom.

The rest of this appendix briefly covers how evangelism is informed by and informs biblical studies, systematic theology, history, ethics and cultural studies. My goal in this is to offer you what my evangelism professor offered me: a way to see how keeping evangelism as our central concern when approaching theological education will strengthen and focus our entire process of theological studies.

BIBLICAL STUDIES

As we navigate evangelism, it is essential that we have a firm grounding in the Bible since it is the primary source from which we learn the good news of what God has done through Jesus Christ. Biblical studies deal with the origin, composition and interpretation of the Bible. Father and son scholars Richard N. Soulen and R. Kendall Soulen explain that this work asks three questions about the Bible and the world, with a variety of critical and interpretive tools to aid in answering each one: (1) Where does the Bible come from? (2) What is the Bible about? (3) Whither does the Bible lead us?[2]

Where does the Bible come from? The first question focuses on the origins of the biblical text. Plumbing the contexts in which the different passages in the Bible were written, it uses tools like source criticism, form criticism, redaction criticism and historical criticism to learn what influenced the writing and composition of the original texts. This includes locating the time and place in which the passage was written, looking for earlier or contemporary extrabiblical literature or oral traditions that may have influenced the text and seeking evidence of ways the author or editor may have utilized sources to create the text.

David Barrett, a scholar who has studied the church's early missionary efforts, has connected this first question of biblical studies with evangelism. Tracing the Greek words that translate to "evangelism" in English, he found their origins in Greco-Roman literature dating to approximately four hundred years before the life of Christ. He concluded that biblical authors appropriated these words to describe sharing the gospel of Jesus Christ because the words were always used in pre-Christian literature to describe something joyful and celebratory.[3] Barrett is bringing the story of where the Bible came from—in this case, the words of the Bible—to bear on our understanding of evangelism.

---

[2]Richard N. Soulen and R. Kendall Soulen, *The Handbook of Biblical Criticism*, 4th ed. (Louisville: Westminster John Knox, 2011).

[3]David B. Barrett, *Evangelize! A Historical Survey of the Concept*, The AD 2000 Series (Birmingham, AL: New Hope, 1987), 79.

What is the Bible about? The second question asks about the content of the Bible. Moving beyond a text's historical location, it asks what the original author's intent was for writing the text. Literary and narrative criticism are part of this work. Walter Klaiber, a New Testament scholar and former United Methodist bishop, is an example of someone answering the second question with a focus on evangelism. He describes overarching themes about evangelism in the Old and New Testaments. In the Old Testament, Klaiber tracks the usage of the Hebrew word *bśr*, which he translates as "bearing good tidings," and concludes that evangelism proclaims God's steadfast love toward people as it relates to their social location. When the people of Israel are suffering under the domination of others, it offers hope

LEARNING ACTIVITY

In his text, Klaiber acknowledges that people can experience even thoughtful and loving evangelism as something that causes suffering. I have used two methods to explore this important observation. The first is to look at the parable of the sower. In the parable we assume that the sower is competent, understanding how to sow the seed in a way that is appropriate to the field in which he is working. Yet even though the seed is sown with all due care, much of it never yields a harvest. Likewise, we need to recognize that we can be as compassionate, loving and sensitive as possible in sharing the good news, but people will respond to it in a variety of ways, including negatively.

The second draws from student experience. Many of us have participated in an intervention with someone who needs to break out of a destructive lifestyle. These interventions are not unlike evangelism. We love the person and want to share the good news that there is a better life for them if they will stop being self-destructive. Yet the message is often received with anger and resentment because the person feels he or she is being judged and condemned. This is a helpful if painful example of how the delivery of good news in a loving, supportive, relationship-connected way can still be seen by someone as a cause of suffering.

by reminding them that God remains faithful to them. In times of celebration, it spurs Israel to give thanks for God's blessings. For those who are marginalized, regardless of whether they are part of the covenant with Israel, it proclaims the good news that God has not forgotten them and will lift them to a better place.[4]

For the New Testament, Klaiber states that evangelism first refers to Jesus proclaiming the good news of the coming kingdom. After the ascension of Jesus, evangelism describes the work of the new church as it invites people to participate in the kingdom through the grace of God made available by Jesus Christ in the power of the Holy Spirit.[5]

Whither does the Bible lead us? The third question of biblical interpretation is concerned with how the text has been received and interpreted over time, including by its original audience and subsequent audiences. This includes some historical and anthropological work to learn about the original audience. It also involves scholars who approach the text from specific perspectives (e.g., feminist or liberationist or Asian). These perspectives are meant to provide interpretations of the text that supplement or rival existing interpretations.

The technical term for the perspective through which we read the Bible is "hermeneutic." Hermeneutics takes both a passive and an active form. The passive form includes the assumptions, values and other ideas we already hold when we encounter the text. These are passive because they are embedded in us by forces apart from our intentionality, such as our cultural and social context.

It is not sufficient for our hermeneutics to be informed only by our pre-existing ideas though. To do this would be to assume that we already have an angel's eye perspective on how to interpret the Bible. This would be a remarkable act of hubris. To avoid this, we must develop an active hermeneutic by being intentional in reflecting on and augmenting the perspectives through which we read the texts. By reading the Bible from different perspectives, we can find new interpretations of the text we could not have seen earlier.

---

[4]Walter Klaiber, *Call and Response: Biblical Foundations of a Theology of Evangelism*, trans. Howard Perry-Trauthig and James A. Dwyer (Nashville: Abingdon, 1997), 21-22.
[5]Ibid., 22-23.

The problem with active hermeneutics is that they can become dogmatic. We can insist that reading the Bible through a particular perspective is the only acceptable way to read it. This is just as wrong as having unexamined passive hermeneutics that influence our interpretations without our noticing it. The remedy for this, as with our passive hermeneutic, is to seek a variety of perspectives, including those we disagree with. In doing this we can keep our own perspective in check by acknowledging the insight other perspectives bring to the interpretive process.

The goal is to have a hermeneutic that provides a consistent and informed process for interpreting the biblical text. This requires self-awareness on our part as we become sensitive to our standing assumptions and as we take into account specific insights that we want to keep in mind as we approach the biblical text. This is important work: The hermeneutics we construct will define what we believe the Bible says.

The need to identify our hermeneutic brings us back to the intersection between evangelism and biblical studies. Since evangelism is a bias for the good news, to read the Bible from the vantage point of evangelism is to read the Bible with a belief that God wants to accomplish good. With this hermeneutic in place, we can read the Bible as a single text that tells the story of how God is working to accomplish good in human history. This is not to suggest that evangelism gives us leave to ignore the historical and social differences in different texts (e.g., how God liberates the Hebrews from Egypt, restores Zion after the Babylonian exile, or offers abundant life through the incarnation, crucifixion and resurrection of Jesus of

---

LEARNING ACTIVITY

A missional hermeneutic can illuminate passages that have long seemed "flat" or inaccessible to us. This is because it brings a different lens to the Bible and offers us new insights into texts we have read many times. A good example of this is reading the Christmas narrative from Luke 2 using a missional hermeneutic. What new insights do we find about the people in the passage? What new insights are there for readers of the passage today? (Hint: In the Greek, the angel greets the shepherds by saying, "Fear not, behold, I evangelize you with great joy.")

Nazareth) but that an evangelistic hermeneutic does not need to view these texts as independent from each other. We can recognize the unique origins and purposes of each while seeing them as part of one story about God working out the good.

Missiologists and biblical scholars have come to recognize the importance of an evangelistic lens for reading and studying the Bible, developing what has become known as a missional hermeneutic. This hermeneutic approaches the Bible with a focus on the mission God is accomplishing.[6] Put another way, it is a reading of Scripture that posits that God has a purpose, and the Scriptures relate how God is carrying out that purpose. Evangelism would supplement this by stating that God's purpose is to accomplish good.

One of the leading scholars in missional hermeneutic is George Hunsberger. Hunsberger argues that there are four elements to reading the Bible with a missional hermeneutic:

1. Recognizing the missional direction of a specific passage by situating it within the larger story of God's mission throughout the Bible.

2. Recognizing the missional locatedness of present-day readers by finding out how their lives intersect with the missional story presented in the Bible. This includes understanding how the Bible's explanations of God's purpose call the readers to participate in God's mission.

3. Recognizing how a passage shapes and equips the reader to participate in God's mission. It is not enough to awaken readers to their calling to participate in God's mission; the Bible also conveys God's promises to those who undertake that mission. Readers can appropriate the living hope these promises offer them as they engage in missional activities.

4. Recognizing how the mission of God should take shape in a specific culture. Drawing on how people in the Bible related to their cultures as they participated in God's mission, readers can find ways to undertake God's mission that are meaningful to their own cultures.[7]

---

[6]Brian D. Russell, "What Is a Missional Hermeneutic?," *Catalyst* (April 1, 2010), www.catalystre sources.org/what-is-a-missional-hermeneutic.

[7]George R. Hunsberger, "Proposals for a Missional Hermeneutic: Mapping a Conversation," *Missiology: An International Review* 39, no. 3 (2011): 309-21.

SYSTEMATIC THEOLOGY

The study of evangelism requires not only that we know the biblical source material of the good news but also that we understand how to explain that material as a coherent whole. Systematic theology provides us with the perspective to do this.

Systematic theology is a field that organizes the beliefs of the Christian faith. It is the job of theology to work through the revelation of God given in the Bible, reflecting on the content and constructing an expression of Christian truth within a given cultural context. How, for example, should Christians value the importance of the dietary laws in the Pentateuch, the commands for justice in the Prophets, and the teachings of Paul about Holy Communion? Systematic theology answers questions like this, providing a coherent vision of the Christian faith.

When a theological tradition is adopted by a branch of the church, the theological constructions of that tradition are formalized as doctrine. Doctrines are authorized teachings of the church. An individual cannot promulgate a doctrine; only a church can. Each branch of the church (Greek Orthodox, Roman Catholic, ELCA, Free Methodist and so on) decides what person or structure is authorized to make doctrinal statements for it. These statements are usually published to let people know the theological stance of that particular church.

Doctrines are often presented independently from one another. There are doctrines that describe what the church believes about God's nature (the doctrine of God), the person of Jesus Christ (Christology), the person of the Holy Spirit (pneumatology), human nature and its relationship to the universe and God (theological anthropology and the doctrine of creation), the problem of evil and sin (hamartiology), God's ultimate purposes (eschatology), how God invites people to participate in those purposes (soteriology), what the church is and how it serves in God's purposes (ecclesiology) and how God mediates the divine presence in specific practices (sacramental theology).

While it's helpful to separate doctrines in order to study them, doctrines are inherently interconnected. Theology is like the spiderweb described in chapter two, with each doctrine forming a strand in that web. We cannot pull on one strand without shifting, skewing or breaking another. To modify our view about any doctrine means rethinking our views of other doctrines.

For example, if we come to believe that Jesus was not fully divine (a position usually called "low Christology"), we must also reconsider our soteriology (if Jesus is only human he cannot heal human nature with his divinity). If we believe that God is waiting for the last few believers to be gathered to heaven before destroying the world and recreating it (a form of eschatology), we will need to adopt a low view of creation (creation becomes a disposable backdrop for God's larger cosmic plan). These are simple examples. The implications for our beliefs would ripple out far beyond the single changes I point to here.

Evangelism helps us see the connections between doctrines in theological traditions, whether those are official traditions taught by branches of the church or not. By insisting that all Christian beliefs point back to the good news of God, we can find the strands that hold the various doctrines together and ascertain how those run through the center point of the good news. More than that, we can discern how the good news is defined and determine if that definition fits with our own authentic belief of what the good news is.

ETHICS

When we reach the point of navigating how our authentic beliefs inform the way we practice evangelism, we need to avoid practices that run counter to the good news we want to share. For example, using a bullhorn to present the Scripture way of salvation on a street corner might be an appropriate practice of evangelism according to our beliefs about the good news (especially for heirs of John Wesley and his field preaching), but it could prove to be a poor practice of evangelism if it comes across as coercive rather than loving to many people. The study of ethics provides us a way to understand and avoid this.

Ethics is the study of structures for making decisions and acting in accordance with those decisions. For example, a work ethic is a framework for making decisions about how we ought to engage in labor. Our work ethic informs how much time, effort and interest, among other things, we invest in our work. While a work ethic focuses on a specific area of life, ethics more generally speaks to our framework for making decisions in all aspects of our lives.

As the study of evangelism requires us to articulate a starting point, ethics requires us to develop a baseline to make decisions. We determine our baseline by looking at the teachings of the Bible, the Christian Tradition and any other tradition (theological or otherwise) we find helpful. In doing this we define what counts as virtue and what counts as vice in a way that is consistent with the canonical and doctrinal teachings of the faith. Armed with this insight, we can make decisions based on a Christian ethic.

Most people think of ethics in terms of one-off decisions (for example, what would you do if a woman came into your office and said her husband wanted the two of them to become swingers, or how would you handle it if a homeless man came to your house one stormy evening and asked to spend the night—both issues I faced when serving as a pastor in a local church). However, ethics is not primarily about answering specific moral questions. Studying ethics is meant to form us so we can live virtuously, no matter how mundane or exotic our lives may be. Such formation is essential for us to practice the good news we preach.

This call to ethical formation resonates with evangelism. The study of evangelism points us to the good news of God as the core of the Christian ethic, affirming as virtuous anything that invites people into the goodness of God and rejecting as vicious anything that denies people participation in God's goodness. If we want to be effective in our evangelism, we will be formed according to this ethical baseline, ordering our daily lives to represent it. We will also develop our evangelistic practices in concert with it.

In *The Ethics of Evangelism*, Elmer Thiessen weighs how the practice of evangelism can be both virtuous and vicious. He concludes that evangelism is virtuous only if it adheres to several criteria:

- It must protect the dignity of those being evangelized.

- It must care for the whole person being evangelized, not just the soul.

- It can use no coercion.

- It can use no psychological manipulation.

- It cannot leverage social power imbalances.

- It cannot induce a person to accept the good news by bribery.

- It cannot sidestep appealing to people rationally.

- It must remain truthful and have integrity.

- It must be humble and make allowances for ambiguity.

- It must be motivated only by love of humanity coupled with love of God.

- It must respect the existing relationships a person being evangelized already has.

- It cannot shame the evangelists if they do not have positive responses to their efforts.

- It is receptive to alternative beliefs presented by the person evangelized.[8]

Thiessen's list is a good one that connects well with what we have already covered. But we should add the need for evangelism to remain authentic to the person practicing it. Nothing kills evangelism faster than hypocrisy. If those we evangelize see that we are not virtuous as defined by our own good news, it will show that we are inauthentic in our practices, claiming to preach the good news of God while acting in a way that is not good. Studies of evangelism and ethics help us guard against this pitfall, the former by prompting us to articulate the good news and the latter calling us to stay virtuous in relationship to that good news.

Bryan Stone, a professor of evangelism, takes this need for ethical formation to its extreme. He suggests that evangelism is defined by the church being ethically formed in a unique way. Highlighting activities that the church engages in (the sacraments, acts of reconciliation), Stone argues that these demonstrate an ethics grounded in the good news of the peaceable kingdom. This makes the church's ethics evangelistic because it invites all people to live in the abundance of God's goodness. Stone contrasts this with every other ethical system the world has to offer, which are built around assumptions of a lack of goodness for all people.[9]

Even if we do not define evangelism entirely in terms of ethics, Stone points us in a helpful direction for studying ethics alongside evangelism. In the face of the problems that wrack their personal lives and the globe alike, people often respond with anguish, resignation and cynicism. As Christians,

---

[8]Elmer John Thiessen, *The Ethics of Evangelism: A Philosophical Defense of Proselytizing and Persuasion* (Downers Grove, IL: InterVarsity Press, 2011), 155-211.
[9]Bryan Stone, *Evangelism After Christendom: The Theology and Practice of Christian Witness* (Grand Rapids: Brazos, 2007), 69-73.

though, we always have hope because of the good news of what God has done through Jesus Christ. If we study ethics in light of this hope, becoming formed by this hope as we study, we will be witnessing to a goodness that many people in the world cannot see. This virtuous hope will be an authentic manifestation of the good news that others might find intriguing and worth their consideration.

HISTORY

History offers a fertile area of study for those of us who are evangelism students. As with the missional hermeneutic in biblical studies, evangelism offers a lens through which we can focus our view of the past. This focus brings with it a trove of insights into how we can navigate evangelism today.

Church history is the most common form of history we encounter in theological education. Often church history is taught as an intellectual history, emphasizing the development of doctrine. We trace how the church determined the earliest doctrines and then reflected on those doctrines over the years. This provides us with a narrative of how the church arrived at the way it articulates the Christian Tradition today. Denominational history supplements this study, teaching us the ways denominational heritages took shape out of the broader intellectual movements of church history.

The unfolding of doctrinal history reveals that we are in a community of Christians that stretches across time as well as space, filled with people who have sought to be honest and clear about their beliefs. We are not alone in working to articulate our faith. Centuries of Christians, including some of the greatest thinkers of all time, struggled to explain what they believed. We have the benefit of being able to stand on their shoulders.

In addition to studying the ideas of the Christians who have come before us, we can learn from how they lived. The saints are our exemplars in this. Their uniquely focused commitment to the good news of God was sufficient to earn them the accolades of the church and sometimes those outside the Christian fold. In becoming acquainted with the saints we develop a more holistic approach to evangelism that gives us a picture of what it means to be formed in the good news. This is why we look to the evangelistic practices of the saints to give us insight into how we develop our own evangelistic practices.

The holistic insights we gain from the saints show that the study of history from the vantage point of evangelism is more than a descriptive enterprise. It is a process of retrieval. We do not just look for who believed what and when. We retrieve articulations and demonstrations of the good news that help us as we learn about the people who embodied those views of the good news. The people who came before us are not just figures from the past but conversation partners who advise and encourage us as we seek to be formed in the good news.

In addition to the intellectual development of doctrine, church history also looks at the past practices of the church. The study of evangelism connects with this by focusing on missionary activities, considering how and why the Christian faith spread around the world. This approach to church history is especially important for missiology, a separate area of study that looks at the mission of God through the church.

A focus on mission history also lets us borrow ideas about practicing evangelism today from what the church has already done. These ideas are especially helpful because we have the benefit of hindsight. We can determine who was involved in the activities—both the evangelists and those being evangelized—the context in which the evangelism took place and the processes that led up to, took place during and followed the evangelistic encounters. We also can see whether the evangelism was effective in the short and long term.

Missiologists and scholars of evangelism alike have sought to mine church history for this kind of insight. Generally, evangelism scholars emphasize specific individuals and their practices, such as St. Patrick and his Celtic Christianity or John Wesley and his class meetings, which can be emulated in the present day. Missiologists look for broader themes and influences that motivated the church to undertake evangelistic work. David Bosch's *Transforming Mission* is a well-recognized text that does this, suggesting that Western church history can be periodized based on how the church organized itself for mission and undertook evangelistic outreach.

A caveat is warranted here: We need to be careful in appropriating the evangelistic work of the past. It is not a simple matter of learning that the church was effective with a practice of evangelism and then adopting that same practice today. The manifold changes that occur over time make this untenable. However, we can learn from the great evangelistic successes as well as the failures of history. We can also look to eras that are analogous to ours to learn which practices might be worth retrieving for today and which should be abandoned before we put any resources toward them. Since there is nothing new under the sun, we can nearly always find lessons in history germane to our situation that will help us navigate evangelism.

History does not drily record the causes and effects of the past; it records the work of the church to embody and share the good news of God in ways we can retrieve and use. History, shaped by the study of evangelism, is an invitation to step into the redemptive work of God and continue the story.

Cultural Studies

Cultural studies are not part of traditional theological education. However, this is beginning to change, with more seminaries and divinity schools requiring at least one course that deals with them. Moreover, the study of evangelism has strong affinities with fields of study that analyze how people live and relate with one another. For this reason, I recommend that those of us who study evangelism include a course that involves cultural analysis.

Like ethics, pursuing cultural studies has to do with how evangelism entails formation. Where ethics points us to the formation we need to remain faithful to the good news we believe, cultural studies show how both we as the evangelists and those we evangelize are formed by how we relate to the people around us. Without the tools to recognize and analyze this, we will be ignorant of a significant factor that influences how we evangelize and how our evangelism is received by others.

A variety of fields are involved with cultural studies. The two most prominent are anthropology and sociology. Anthropology studies civilizations by researching the cultural, linguistic, biological and archaeological evidence associated with a particular group of people. From this it seeks to explain how people in that civilization lived in the past and, if the civilization is extant, how they live today. Sociology looks at the structure and behaviors of a current group of people, including the impact on that behavior by factors like race, gender, age, geographical location and socioeconomic standing.

As evangelism students, we can draw from both anthropology and sociology, especially when we begin navigating to the ways we will practice evangelism. Both fields teach us about the contexts that formed us as well as who we will be evangelizing so we can tailor our practices to suit them.

In 1963 Louis Luzbetak, a Catholic missiologist, argued that anthropology should be part of the study of missions and evangelism. Anthropologically astute evangelists would be able to (1) create linkages between core Christian beliefs and the values and assumptions at the core of a culture, (2) demonstrate how Christian expectations were consistent with some of the expectations and beliefs already in a culture and (3) develop reciprocity between Christian and native cultural practices and beliefs so that there could be greater integration between the two.[10] With these skills, the evangelist could make the good news less alien to a new culture and ameliorate the cultural barriers people might feel in accepting it.

The scholars involved with the Gospel and Our Culture Network (gocn .org) have sought to do this anthropological work, focusing on providing a savvy cultural analysis of North America. Their publications and meetings offer some of the best biblical and anthropological thinking available to those who want to bring the good news to people living in the United States and Canada.

Where anthropology opens the door for us to relate our good news to the core values of a people, sociology allows us to relate to the people themselves. By gaining insight into the motivations, activities and relational structures held by a specific group of people, we can develop methods for sharing the good news that are sensitive to the ways people are used to operating. Without this sociological information we end up developing evangelistic practices that may suit our tastes but are inaccessible, unintelligible or offensive to those we are trying to reach.

Evangelistic use of sociology is most common today in church growth and outreach literature, which presents a variety of ways we can invite people to participate in our communities of faith. These ready-made explanations of how we can relate to "unchurched Harry and Mary" can be helpful; however, we do not need to rely on existing sociological analyses to

---

[10]Louis J. Luzbetak, "Toward an Applied Missionary Anthropology," *Anthropological Quarterly* 34, no. 4 (2003): 165-76.

refine our evangelistic practices. We can make use of sociological research by becoming familiar with the primary data about a group of people and forming our own conclusions.

Demographics and psychographics are two sets of sociological data that are helpful for evangelism students to understand. Demographics describe the exterior traits of people, such as their race, language spoken, ethnic origin or age. Psychographics describe the deeper beliefs, values and feelings of a group of people.

Demographics help us think through the initial issues we will face when we evangelize a group of people. There could be more or fewer of these issues depending on how great the demographic differences are between us and the group we want to reach. For example, an immigrant church that wants to reach out to its largely non-immigrant neighborhood will have to overcome more demographic hurdles than a congregation that is largely made up of the same ethnic group as the people in the neighborhood.

Psychographics give us clues as to what activities would make our evangelism most attractive. If we find out that people who live where we want to evangelize are concerned with having access to quality childcare because both parents have to work, this is a need we could consider meeting to demonstrate the love of God to the people and their children.

The best way to gather both anthropological and sociological data is to do field research. This means we need to

LEARNING ACTIVITY

There are a number of places we can go to gather demographic and psychographic information. Demographic data is often free and online. Government records (especially from the US Census Bureau) and some university studies often have relatively up-to-date and accessible demographics. Psychographic data, because it requires additional research, usually must be purchased. There are companies that will do psychographic research in a specific geographical area and then sell it to church leaders. Often denominational judicatories have relationships with one of these companies, allowing individual congregations or pastors to access data for free or for a nominal cost.

go to the place we want to do evangelism and meet the people there. The formal studies of anthropology and sociology will equip us with the tools we need to gather and interpret the data from our research.

There is one important warning those of us who undertake cultural analysis as part of our evangelism studies need to heed. Evangelism is not just about using data to increase numbers. Focusing on attracting people to a congregation rather than on inviting them to claim the good news leads to the kind of negative evangelism practices we should avoid. The same thing happens if we are learning about the people only so that we can find ways to shape them into our own cultural and social norms. Avoiding these dangers requires constant vigilance.

Evangelism as a Nexus Point in Theological Education

I remember my first few minutes of seminary like it happened yesterday, but I do not remember much of what happened after that. The next two years are a muddle of frustration and anger on my part. I felt as if my faith was assaulted on multiple fronts as I entered each course.

What I wish I had known then was that I did not need to run up and down the entire line of my beliefs, trying to ward off the doubts raised by my studies. Instead I could have articulated my belief in the good news, which would have given me a solid foundation from which to encounter the new ideas I was hearing. It would have given me a sense for what questions I needed to ask of each new subject I encountered so I could learn from it rather than feeling attacked by it. It would also have shown me how the individual subjects knit together academically and in relation to my life as a Christian.

The study of evangelism stands as the nexus point in the midst of theological education, both being informed by and informing these already interwoven fields of study. This calls those of us who study evangelism to be excellent students in all the fields of theological education. In gaining familiarity with these fields, we gain the capacity to discern and articulate our beliefs. As excellent students who focus on evangelism, we also are able to form the other fields so that they are better able to convey the good news of God.

How to Use
This Book

I want to reach two audiences with this book: those who teach evangelism and those who study evangelism, regardless of whether they carry out these activities in seminaries, divinity schools or the local church. The bulk of this book is for students. It offers them a framework for studying evangelism that will help order their own thinking about the Christian faith and guide them in turning their beliefs into evangelistic practices. For those studying evangelism as part of a larger curriculum, the appendix offers a detailed look at how the study of evangelism intersects with the primary fields they will encounter in theological education.

For teachers of evangelism, the book is supplemented with online material they can use in course preparation. The book provides a short, accessible introduction to evangelism along with a framework for introducing specific authors and theories. The online material includes sample syllabi, a discussion of how the pedagogy of evangelism operates in both face-to-face and online teaching environments, and a set of links to other online sources. For teachers in local churches, the online material also includes a sample retreat schedule for leading small groups through the material in the book and a modified SWOT (strengths, weaknesses, opportunities, threats) analysis tool for diagnosing a local church's (or even a specific ministry's) evangelistic effectiveness.

FOR TEACHERS OF EVANGELISM IN THEOLOGICAL EDUCATION
This text was several years in the making, coming both from my experiences teaching evangelism in seminaries and from working with congregational

and denominational officials on evangelism strategies. It encapsulates the insights I have gained from these interactions and has been informed by the feedback of countless students.

Perhaps the most surprising realization I had when I started teaching evangelism was the inability of many students and church leaders to articulate what they believed. Sadly, this state of affairs has not improved over time. In part this has to do with poor catechetical training in our local churches. We have raised a generation that knows they are Christian only in a vague sense of the term and are without the vocabulary and concepts to explain what being Christian means. This is especially dangerous because this same generation is now coming of age as the new leaders of our congregations and denominations. If we do not intervene, their lack of articulation will pass along to the generation after them as the accepted standard for Christian identity.

I think this inability to articulate what we believe comes from wanting to avoid upsetting the careful balance of what is often called "diversity" in mainline circles. In truth, this diversity is not so much a celebration of people with their unique cultures, perspectives and ways of sharing the goodness of God as it is a hush policy that demands unity at the cost of any deep engagement with each other that might lead to theological disagreement. In such an environment, personal formation in faith through study, devotions or any other means is discouraged. It is better to maintain a surface-level faith that conforms to whatever generic understanding of Christianity is in vogue at the moment than to rock the already fragile boats of the denominational institutions.

This is not to suggest that students and others are uninterested in claiming their Christian identities more fully. In the absence of a distinct process of Christian formation, they grasp at political, social or other causes that help them explain who they are and what they believe as followers of Jesus Christ. This makes matters worse rather than better. Mimicking the shrill discourse of the media, this approach is polarizing within a seminary or congregation, and it tends to raise the cultural and social issues of the day to the level of *status confessionis*, since these are the primary issues people can use to explain their faith in a way that is intelligible to the larger culture.

All of this affects how we teach evangelism. Historically, evangelism courses and literature have been toolkits, explaining the best practices for inviting others to become Christians. However, if we have no clarity about what we believe, we cannot start our teaching by discussing the tactics of how to invite people to believe along with us. Instead we must start with an assumption that the people we are teaching—even those considered advanced in their faith—need time and space to discern what they really believe (authenticity) and to become proficient with the Christian concepts and vocabulary (articulation) so they can explain what they believe. Only after all this background work is done can we move to discussing practices of evangelism.

What helps us in this process is the fact that all people have some core beliefs and experiences in reference to God. We can use these as a starting point to help students begin to articulate their authentic Christian beliefs.

I recognize that starting with students' personal experiences can be seen as a weaker move than inculcating them with specific doctrines. But I make this move because many of those we teach are starting with little background engagement with classical doctrine or the Bible. This means that if we start by insisting on these sources as the entry to evangelism, we face the doubly hard challenge of calling students to value them while also trying to teach them the material connected to evangelism. More than that, we will inevitably imprint our specific perspectives on these sources. This will further complicate our teaching by forcing our students to struggle not just with the sources themselves but with our interpretations of those sources. Our students may not be experts on the Bible or doctrine, but they certainly do have opinions on how those sources are interpreted!

We cannot assume a common understanding or even valuation of the Bible and doctrine among our students. However, we can assume that all our students have experiences of the goodness of God. Moreover, these experiences belong authentically to the students. These experiences become the pedagogical hook on which we can help the students hang what they learn as we prepare them to articulate their faith with others.

Having grown up in a theologically conservative congregation, I admit that even I am uncomfortable with my own work at times. Part of me would like to approach evangelism based on classical Christology. However, having also spent many years serving as a pastor and a professor in a mainline denomination, I know doing that makes reaching across the theological spectrum harder. People are less inclined today to hear different beliefs than they are to hear each other's stories of how they came to belief.

My hope is that by introducing evangelism through equipping students to articulate their authentic beliefs about the Christian faith, I will give students the foundation to share their stories. This will lay the foundation not only for students to share their faith outside the church but to share their faith within the church. I believe that evangelism serves as the entry point to forming the generous natures we need for genuine diversity and unity in the church.

Since evangelism brings our theology to the fore, let me say a word about me. I am ordained in the United Methodist Church. Theologically I follow closely in the footsteps of John Wesley, the founder of the Methodist revival. In early twenty-first-century nomenclature that would put me in the evangelical camp though with soteriological emphases on grace and scriptural holiness that would differentiate me from those in the same camp with a Reformed background. One of the primary ways you will see this emphasis is in my insistence on holding evangelism and formation together rather than treating them independently. For Wesley, salvation was a lifelong process of growing in grace, meaning that the invitation to enter the life of God through Jesus Christ never ended. This means that we are evangelizing just as surely when we are sharing the gospel with someone for the first time as we are when we welcome long-standing saints of God to a deeper faith. It also means that I believe we are called to offer God's salvation both to individuals and to whole groups of people (tribes, nation-states, churches and any other organization of people). Evangelism entails both the call for individual conversion and the call for a holy culture and society.

Occasionally you will find learning activities in text boxes throughout the book. These are exercises, assignments and other tools I use to teach evangelism in my own courses. I have found all of these to be effective in helping students discern and articulate their faith. Remember also to check the online teaching material connected to the book.

FOR CHURCH LEADERS

As I have had the privilege of working alongside churches across the United States and internationally, I have found this model for teaching evangelism to be useful on both the local and denominational levels. There are several reasons for this:

1. It offers a way into what can often be an uncomfortable conversation in local churches. As someone who has served as a pastor, I know the awkwardness around evangelism and all the ancillary concerns that come from it. I also know the desire pastors have to invite their congregations into a hopeful and joyful discussion of evangelism. This book gives pastors tools for entering this conversation with their people.

2. It is accessible to lay and clergy leaders. Since most seminary students are not clergy until after they graduate, this material is geared toward laity. It does not assume that those using it have a formal theological background. However, it can scale to match whatever level of theological sophistication people may have, so clergy or more advanced laity will find it just as useful.

3. It is meant to be catechetical. Evangelism requires people to reflect on what they believe about God and why they believe it. It then calls on them to articulate these beliefs. This process can be used to help Christians claim the core Christian beliefs and values in their own words—something that is difficult to do without a framework.

4. It does not adhere to a specific theology. Seminaries often draw students from across a theological spectrum. In order to make evangelism something that all students can claim, I developed this approach to accommodate whatever theology people may bring to it. As such, all congregations can make use of this book.

5. It leads to practical action. Since the mid-twentieth century there has been a division between the so-called scholars and practitioners of evangelism. Usually I am lumped with the former group since I am on faculty at a seminary. However, I spent twelve years serving in local churches, including as a youth pastor, associate pastor and solo pastor. I developed this model to include intellectual work around theology but also to generate practices that put flesh on that theology. I want to honor the hard-working ministers who care about their theology but who also need a matrix to translate their ideas into actions.

I do skew toward addressing students engaged in formal theological education at times because that is my own setting. If you move past that, you will find a solid process that will serve you well in your ministry setting. The chapter on practice will be especially helpful for you, as it briefly covers the core points discussed in the previous chapters with an eye on how to turn our Christian belief in the good news into action. Moreover, there is a study guide available online to help you lead your congregation or small group through this book.

I commend this book to you and hope you will find it useful in reclaiming evangelism as a word you can use and a practice you can undertake in your congregations. Please let me know of successes or struggles you have with navigating evangelism. Also, I would very much like to know of any improvements or alterations you have made to the navigation model so it can be more effective in your church.

Index

Finding the Textbook You Need

The IVP Academic Textbook Selector
is an online tool for instantly finding the IVP books
suitable for over 250 courses across 24 disciplines.

www.ivpress.com/academic/